Short on Time, Long on Learning

Activities for Those Teachable Moments

Mary Northrup

A Publication of THE BOOK REPORT & LIBRARY TALK
Professional Growth Series

Linworth Publishing, Inc.
Worthington, Ohio

Library of Congress Cataloging-in-Publication Data

Northrup, Mary.
    Short on time, long on learning : activities for those teachable moments / Mary Northrup.
        p. cm.
    Includes indexes.
    ISBN 0-938865-99-4
1. Education, Elementary—Activity programs—Handbooks, manuals, etc. 2. Elementary
    school libraries—Activity programs—Handbooks, manuals, etc. I. Title.

    LB1592 .N67 2000
    372.13—dc21

                                             00-055874

Published by Linworth Publishing, Inc.
480 East Wilson Bridge Road, Suite L
Worthington, Ohio 43085

Series Information:
      From The Professional Growth Series

ISBN 0-938865-99-4

5 4 3 2 1

Table of Contents

Table of Contents continued

Table of Contents continued

Table of Contents continued

Table of Contents continued

Table of Contents continued

About the Author

Mary Northrup is a librarian and writer. She has written articles and puzzles for LIBRARY TALK, THE BOOK REPORT, *Calliope*, *Cobblestone*, *AppleSeeds*, *Turtle*, and many other magazines for children. She is the author of the children's book *American Computer Pioneers*. A former teacher, Northrup has worked in public, academic, and special libraries, and she is currently Reference Librarian at Maple Woods Community College, Kansas City, Missouri. She lives with her husband and two children in Missouri.

Introduction

Short on Time, Long on Learning provides a wealth of activities for fourth, fifth, and sixth grade teachers to use in those spare moments when wasted minutes can be transformed into educational experiences. Those times when papers are being collected, roll is called, before lunch, or between lessons are ideal opportunities to review, enrich, or prepare for new material. Librarians, too, can use many of the activities while waiting for a teacher to return or for a group to finish. Those activities especially suitable for librarians are indicated with a ★. See Appendix A for a complete listing of these activities.

The activities in this book range from individual paper-and-pencil games, to partner activities, to whole-class ideas, and combinations thereof. Each activity indicates how many students may participate. The activities are arranged within each subject by level of participation. Class activities are listed first under each subject; activities for partners and individuals follow. Reproducible sheets for individual activities are provided at the end of the chapters.

For those students who seek a higher level, some of the activities include a "Challenge," which provides an additional spur to learning.

The index at the back of the book provides links to curriculum.

Learning truly can take place every minute of the day. This book is presented in the hope that your students will have fun, retain what is learned, and become open to new learning. Make the most of those moments!

 Language Arts

A WIN BY ANY OTHER NAME

■ **PARTICIPATION:** Class

■ **MATERIALS:** large sheet of paper and marker

How to Play!

Ask the students to collect examples of various words used to describe sports victories or defeats from the newspaper, radio, and TV. Make a list.

CHALLENGE: Imagine if other contests were covered like sports events. How could victories be described in matches between chess players, moviemakers, writers, inventors?

★ I'M THINKING OF . . . .

■ **PARTICIPATION:** Class

How to Play!

One student describes an object to the class, without giving it away, in five sentences. Others guess what the object is.

MEMORY BANK

■ **PARTICIPATION:** Class

■ **MATERIALS:** paper and pencil

■ **ADVANCE PREPARATION:** On the board, write a list of 10 words from a lesson that day.

How to Play!

Present the list to the class. Allow them time to study the words—about 20 seconds. Then cover the words and have the class write down the ones they remember.

CHALLENGE: Use a list of unrelated words.

CONCENTRATION

PARTICIPATION: Class

MATERIALS: paper and tape

ADVANCE PREPARATION: Write a list of words on the board that contains pairs of synonyms. On each piece of paper, write a number. Tape a piece of paper over each word on the board.

How to Play!

Students take turns selecting two pieces of paper to flip over and see if they match. If they do, remove the paper covers.

COMMUNICATION IS THE KEY

PARTICIPATION: Class

MATERIALS: large paper or poster board and marker

How to Play!

Make a class list, "Ways We Communicate." Think of both natural and machine-made ways.

SOLUTION ON PAGE 134.

SIGN IT

PARTICIPATION: Class

MATERIALS: books on sign language

ADVANCE PREPARATION: Review the books to learn some basic words in sign language.

How to Play!

Demonstrate some words in sign language. Have students try. Add more signs over several days and weeks.

★ ONE-ACT

PARTICIPATION: Class

MATERIALS: anything in the classroom

How to Play!

Act out a section of a story the class has just read.

★ TIME TRAVEL

■ **PARTICIPATION:** Class

How to Play!

Select one character from a story the class has read and imagine him or her in another time or place. Discuss.

LOOK IT UP

ESCUELA!

■ **PARTICIPATION:** Class/Partners

■ **MATERIALS:** foreign language dictionaries

How to Play!

Look up one familiar English word in each dictionary; for example, "school." Write the various foreign words on the board. Compare.

CHALLENGE: Look up and compare words that are related, such as "mother" and "father," "girl" and "boy," "aunt" and "uncle," days of the week, or seasons.

ON/OFF, IN/OUT

■ **PARTICIPATION:** Class/Partners

■ **MATERIALS:** 3 by 5 cards (or larger) and pen or marker

■ **ADVANCE PREPARATION:** Write one word on each card. Each word must have a common antonym.

How to Play!

Hand out a card to each student. The student must present the word on the card to the class and think of an antonym for it.

CHALLENGE: The student must also give a synonym for the word.

NATIONAL CELEBRATION MONTH

- **PARTICIPATION:** Class/Partners
- **MATERIALS:** *Chase's Calendar of Events*

How to Play!

Find out what month or week it is (e.g., National Peanut Month, Astronomy Week). Make up your own special event, tying it into the curriculum.

★ CAN YOU?

- **PARTICIPATION:** Class/Partners/Individuals

How to Play!

Either in writing or orally, describe:

	without using the word:
sun	*round*
bus	*large, big*
fire	*hot*
egg	*shell*
rock	*hard*
water	*wet*
book	*pages*
music	*sound*
glass	*clear*
calendar	*numbers*

★ MIX IT UP

- **PARTICIPATION:** Class/Partners/Individuals
- **MATERIALS:** paper and pencil
- **ADVANCE PREPARATION:** Write a phrase on the board—for example, the title of a read-aloud book, a favorite saying or proverb, the closest upcoming holiday.

How to Play!

How many words can be made from its letters?

REPORTER

■ **PARTICIPATION:** Class/Individuals

■ **MATERIALS:** a collection of newspaper stories

■ **ADVANCE PREPARATION:** Cut out stories from the newspaper that may be of interest to the students.

How to Play!

Discuss the who, what, where, when, and why (or 5 W's) in newspaper stories. Have students present one of the stories to the class, reading the first few sentences and telling which words or phrases illustrate the 5 W's.

★ HAPPILY EVER AFTER?

■ **PARTICIPATION:** Class/Individuals

■ **MATERIALS:** paper and pencil

How to Play!

Instruct the students to write a new ending for a story they have just read.

WRITE THE RIGHT ONE

■ **PARTICIPATION:** Class/Individuals

■ **MATERIALS:** paper and pencil

How to Play!

As a class, write a list of homonyms on the board. Then have the students make up sentences containing two or more homonyms.

QUICK, THINK!

■ **PARTICIPATION:** Partners

■ **MATERIALS:** paper and pencil

How to Play!

One student says a word, and the other student writes down the first word that comes to mind. Use lists of descriptive words, familiar objects in the classroom, spelling words, or word lists from other subjects.

 CHALLENGE: The word that is written must be longer than the word that is said.

SOMETHING'S MISSING

■ PARTICIPATION: Partners

■ MATERIALS: paper and pencil

How to Play!

One student writes a sentence, leaving out all vowels. The other student must fill in the blanks to complete the sentence.

CHALLENGE: One student writes a sentence with no consonants; partner fills in the blanks.

MEMORY BUILDER

■ PARTICIPATION: Partners

■ MATERIALS: paper and pencil

How to Play!

One student writes a word, the other one looks at it, memorizes it, and says it when it is covered. Then the first student writes another word to add to the first, and the partner looks, memorizes, and says both words when they are covered. Continue until the second student cannot remember all the words. Take a tally from each group of how many words could be remembered.

CHALLENGE: Make each set of words different, rather than adding from the first.

IT'S NEW! IT'S DIFFERENT!

■ PARTICIPATION: Partners/Individuals

■ MATERIALS: paper and crayons or markers

■ ADVANCE PREPARATION: Cut out some ads from newspapers or magazines. Make a note of ad phrases that you've heard on TV.

How to Play!

Challenge students to think of ad jingles, phrases, or catchwords (in print or from TV). Have them write an ad using these for a product that is something they would use.

CHALLENGE: Write an ad for a totally new product. It can be potentially real or imaginary.

PUZZLE THIS OUT

- **PARTICIPATION:** Individuals
- **MATERIALS:** graph paper and pencil

How to Play!

Students will make a simple crossword puzzle (just a few words across and down), using words about a subject they love or are now studying.

CHALLENGE: Make the puzzle bigger and more tightly connected.

IMAGINATIVE SIMILES

- **PARTICIPATION:** Individuals
- **MATERIALS:** paper and pencil
- **ADVANCE PREPARATION:** Write the following phrases on the board:

cold as	busy as
fresh as	dry as
black as	blue as
green as	new as
easy as	smooth as

How to Play!

It's not hard to fall into a rut with similes. They can easily become cliches, such as "cold as ice," or "fresh as a daisy." Have students complete the phrases as creatively as possible.

TOUGH RHYMES

■ **PARTICIPATION:** Individuals

■ **MATERIALS:** paper and pencil

■ **ADVANCE PREPARATION:** List the following words on the board:

tough	taught
shine	do
though	soar
write	straight
sheet	rule

How to Play!

Have the students write a rhyming word for each that does not have the same ending spelling. (Example: for "tough," "stuff" is allowed, "rough" is not.)

SOLUTION ON PAGE 134.

UC

■ **PARTICIPATION:** Individuals

■ **MATERIALS:** paper and pencil

How to Play!

On the board, write letters of the alphabet that sound like or could be used for words. Challenge the students to think of other letters that could be used. Here are some hints:

A	a		O	owe, oh
B	bee, be		P	pea
C	see, sea		Q	queue
D	the		R	are
F	if		S	is
G	gee		T	tea
I	I, eye		U	ewe, you
J	jay		Y	why
N	in			

Next, have them use the letters to make a sentence. (Simple: UC = you see.
Complex: Y S D U N D C? = Why is the ewe in the sea?)

★ BOX OFFICE SMASH!

■ PARTICIPATION: Individuals

■ MATERIALS: paper and pencil

How to Play!

After viewing a video or filmstrip, have students write a short review, complete with stars, or thumbs up/down, and so on.

A SENSE-IBLE THING

■ PARTICIPATION: Individuals

■ MATERIALS: paper and pencil

How to Play!

Have the students write a sentence for each direction:

Describe a taste.
Describe a smell.
Describe a visual scene.
Describe a sound.
Describe a feeling.

Then discuss: Which is easiest? Most difficult?

★ INTRODUCING . . .

■ PARTICIPATION: Class

How to Play!

Read a short biography of an author. Here are some sources: *Lives of the Writers* by Kathleen Krull (Harcourt, 1994), *Who and When series* by Sarah Halliwell (Raintree/Steck-Vaughn, 1998), *Twenty Names in Modern Literature* by Edwina Connor (Marshall Cavendish, 1988). Ask your librarian for more suggestions.

CAPITALIZE ON THIS

- **PARTICIPATION:** Class/Individuals
- **MATERIALS:** paper and pencil

How to Play!

As a class, make a list on the board of situations where capitals are needed (e.g., book and movie titles, the first word of a sentence, days of the week, months of the year, proper names, brand names, names of continents, countries, states and cities, names of groups or organizations, the names of tribes and nationalities). Have students come up with an example of each.

★ ALL THE PARTS

- **PARTICIPATION:** Class
- **MATERIALS:** a variety of books

How to Play!

Show a book, opening to each part and asking students to identify these parts: title page, copyright page, table of contents, index, glossary, and so on. Discuss why certain parts might be included in some books and not others.

PARTS OF SPEECH SCRAMBLE

How to Play!

The letters are all mixed up! Unscramble them to name the part of speech that is shown in the examples.

EXAMPLES	PARTS OF SPEECH	
under, from, by	soopernitip	_____
hike, became, has listened	berv	_____
and, but, or	nuccijotnon	_____
dog, Washington, baseball	unno	_____
loudly, quietly, perfectly	braved	_____
she, you, their	noropun	_____
hooray! oh! ugh!	jertcinintoe	_____
a, an, the	crealit	_____
tiny, colorful, best	tiedvejac	_____

SOLUTION ON PAGE 134.

ALL ALLITERATION

Is it possible to write a sentence in which every word begins with the same letter? It's fun to try! Finish each sentence with a word beginning with the same letter as the other words in the sentence.

An alligator ate _____.

Bonnie's bouncing baby _____.

Curt can _____.

Drowsy dogs _____.

Eight eggs _____.

Four furry foxes _____.

Gary galloped _____.

Has Hanna _____?

I invited _____.

Jenny jumped _____.

Kangaroos kick _____.

Leaping leopards _____.

Many miners make _____.

Noble Nate nodded _____.

Observe old _____.

Patrick's poodles _____.

Quick queens _____.

Robert returned _____.

Seven scissors _____.

The thief thanked _____.

Una urged, "Use _____."

Villagers view _____.

Walter waves _____.

Xerxes x-rayed _____.

You yelled _____.

Zany zebras _____.

CHALLENGE: Use more than one word (all with the same beginning letter) to complete the sentence. What is a good reference book to use if you're stuck?

LETTER BY LETTER

How to Play!

From the letters below, make as many words as you can. But here is the rule: The letters must be next to or diagonal to each other as you use them; for example, in the first set below, PET is allowed, TUB is not because the U is not next to or diagonal to both the T and the B.

1

```
M  U  N
T  E  D
P  T  B
```

2

```
I  R  W
N  A  T
C  H  P
```

3

```
Y  O  S
J  U  T
D  M  P
```

4

```
B  A  T  L
O  H  I  H
T  G  W  R
U  N  E  C
```

5

```
S  C  R  N
H  T  A  E
A  U  M  O
I  N  T  D
```

6

```
T  N  E  I
B  E  V  N
I  U  M  A
Q  G  R  F
```

SOLUTION ON PAGE 135.

How to Play!

A library is an orderly place, but the words below are all mixed up. Can you help sort them out?

At the library, you can find <u>sokob</u>, <u>smazeagin</u>, <u>snepepwars</u>, <u>dovies</u>, <u>speat</u>, and <u>frolicmim</u>.

_____   _____   _____

_____   _____   _____

The books are divided into <u>tocnifi</u> (which tells a made-up story), and <u>finticnono</u> (which is true).

_____   _____

To find these books, use the <u>lagacot</u>.   _____

With it, you can look up books by <u>orutha</u> (the person who wrote the book), <u>litet</u> (the name of the book), or <u>becsjut</u> (what the book is about).

_____   _____   _____

The books are on the <u>slevesh</u>.   _____

Nonfiction books have <u>lalc brunsme</u>, which use the <u>yeDwe cladime</u> system.

_____   _____

If you need help, the <u>rilbriana</u> will help you.   _____

You need a <u>yarlrib drac</u> to borrow books.   _____

Bring them back on time or you may have to pay a <u>nefi</u>.   _____

Sometimes libraries have special <u>spragmor</u> for kids.   _____

SOLUTION ON PAGE 135.

★ GET YOUR ANSWERS HERE

Who was the tallest person ever?   dictionary

Where is a list of the presidents in order?   phone book

How do you pronounce "zoology"?   almanac

What states border on Canada?   encyclopedia

Where can I get my hair cut?   *Guinness Book of World Records*

Where can I find out about planets?   atlas

SOLUTION ON PAGE 135.

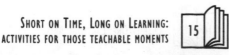

How to Play!

Books can be fiction, which is a made-up story, or nonfiction, which is true. In the pairs below, one book is fiction and the other is nonfiction. Circle the F for fiction or the NF for nonfiction.

F **NF** *The Adventures of Tom Sawyer*
F **NF** A book about the author's experiences rafting down a river

F **NF** A sports statistics book
F **NF** A story about a hockey team that exists in the author's imagination

F **NF** A book about Alaska, its geography, history, and people
F **NF** An adventure story set in the Arctic Circle

F **NF** A novel about an astronaut
F **NF** A guide to star-gazing

F **NF** A travel guide to Disney World
F **NF** A story with Mickey Mouse as the main character

F **NF** A biography of Queen Elizabeth I
F **NF** A time travel story in which a girl goes back to the 1500s

F **NF** A book about a dog that talks
F **NF** An animal encyclopedia

F **NF** A how-to-draw book
F **NF** A book in which the main character draws scenes that come to life

SOLUTION ON PAGE 136.

LOOK! NO VOWELS!

How to Play!

Many words in English do not contain any of the five main vowels—a, e, i, o, or u. Use the clues below to discover some of these words.

It makes a trio with gold and frankincense _____

A good question to ask to find out things_____

Gnats do this; so do 747's _____

She may tell your good fortune _____

A Greek god's or goddess' story _____

A place to lift weights and do exercises _____

A way to cook _____

One of a short tribe _____

A desert, a non-rainy day, or a type of humor _____

The "beat" of music _____

 CHALLENGE: Can you think of more words that do not include an a, e, i, o, or u?

SOLUTION ON PAGE 136.

★ HANS CHRISTIAN ANDERSEN

Hans Christian Andersen was born in Denmark. As a boy, he liked to make up stories. He went to school, but still could not read or write when he was a teenager. He went back to school at 17 and later became the writer of some of the most famous fairy tales in the world.

How to Play!

Unscramble the underlined words below to make the title of a Hans Christian Andersen tale.

The Little raMdime   _____

The Ugly luDginck   _____

The cresPsin and the Pea   _____

The Little thaMc Girl   _____

The Emperor's New tleChso   _____

The nwoS Queen   _____

The Steadfast Tin ridleSo   _____

blunTamhie   _____

The eRd Shoes   _____

The Fir reTe   _____

SOLUTION ON PAGE 136.

ON YOUR MARK

How to Play!

Hidden in the puzzle are some punctuation words. They may appear across, down, backward, or diagonally. Use the list below to help you. Then write the letters that are left for a message.

```
S K R A M N O I T A T O U Q D P
I L D Y O O U K N O W T U H A A
A T A L T N E H P Y H E H S E R
S M O S O S T H C O S M M E O E
T C N L H E A T P T T E R M I N
E X C L A M A T I O N P O I N T
R N T H M E A O L D R P H C A H
I B H O E T N F O O U T N O D E
S I C S N M E N G I L I S L S S
K H W O A N G I S R A L L O D E
R D S R I D S T H E E L E N P S
T T K D N A S R E P M A E R E A
```

DASH	HYPHEN	SEMICOLON	QUESTION MARK
COLON	PERIOD	APOSTROPHE	QUOTATION MARKS
COMMA	ASTERISK	DOLLAR SIGN	EXCLAMATION POINT
SLASH	AMPERSAND	PARENTHESES	

__ __ __ __   __ __ __   __ __ __   __ __ __ __ __

__ __ __ __   __ __ __   __ __ __ __   __ __ __

__ __ __   __ __ __ __ __   __ __ __ __ __

__ __ __ __   __ __ __ __   __ __ __   __ __ __

__ __ __ __ __ __   __ __ _?

SOLUTION ON PAGE 137.

CHAPTER **2**

 Social Studies

SHORT, BUT TO THE POINT

■ **PARTICIPATION:** Class

■ **MATERIALS:** an almanac, encyclopedia, or the book *State Names, Seals, Flags, and Symbols* by Benjamin F. Shearer and Barbara S. Shearer (Greenwood, 1994)

■ **ADVANCE PREPARATION:** Write the motto of your state on the board.

How to Play!

Discuss briefly what a motto is and who has one. Come up with a motto for the class.

 CHALLENGE: Make up a motto for your school if it does not already have one, or for individuals.

CELEBRATE!

■ **PARTICIPATION:** Class

■ **MATERIALS:** large sheet of paper and marker

How to Play!

As a class, make a list of as many holidays as you can.

ONE HUNDRED YEARS

■ **PARTICIPATION:** Class

How to Play!

Discuss what century we are in now. What century was the Civil War (or any other historic event you are studying) in? Say a date, or have a student say one; others must identify the century.

 CHALLENGE: Think of B.C. dates. Identify the century.

GEOGRAPHICAL KNOW-HOW

PARTICIPATION: Class

MATERIALS: detailed map of your state or the United States that can be written on

How to Play!

Using a compass, draw a circle around your city on the map. Find cities of a similar size in the circle. How are they shown? Find larger cities and smaller cities.

 CHALLENGE: Find cities students have been to. Identify size.

EVERYONE WAS YOUNG ONCE

PARTICIPATION: Class

How to Play!

Select one character from the time period you are studying in history. Discuss what that person's life as a child must have been like. Consider clothing, toys, food, education, parental occupations and responsibilities, home, and chores.

CHANGE IT, PLEASE

PARTICIPATION: Class

MATERIALS: business section of a newspaper showing currency exchange rates

How to Play!

Study the exchange rates. Make up some amounts to exchange into pesos, lira, marks, francs, and so on.

CHALLENGE: Change between countries (other than the United States), for example, francs for marks.

WHEN WAS THAT?

PARTICIPATION: Class

ADVANCE PREPARATION: Draw a time line on the board.

How to Play!

Students must take a list of five events and put them in the right order on the line. Use events from a time you have studied or are studying.

CONCENTRATION

■ **PARTICIPATION:** Class

■ **MATERIALS:** pieces of paper and tape

■ **ADVANCE PREPARATION:** Write numbers on paper. Write the names of countries and their capitals on the board, in mixed-up order. Cover with paper taped to board.

How to Play!

Students guess the correct country and its capital, as paper is removed.

★ WHO WILL IT BE?

■ **PARTICIPATION:** Class

■ **MATERIALS:** large sheet of paper and marker

How to Play!

Make a list, as a class, of the top 10 most important people in the past century. Be prepared to defend your choice.

★ THAT WILL WORK

■ **PARTICIPATION:** Class

■ **MATERIALS:** large sheet of paper and marker

How to Play!

As a class, make a list of the top inventions of the past century.

CHALLENGE: Make a list of the top inventions of the past millennium.

NAME THAT CONTINENT

■ **PARTICIPATION:** Class

■ **MATERIALS:** map or globe

How to Play!

Teacher calls out names of countries. Students must name the continent where each country is located. If students are stumped, the teacher can point out the continents on the map or globe.

IT'S A REGIONAL THING

■ **PARTICIPATION:** Class

■ **MATERIALS:** map of the continental United States with the regions highlighted as follows:

Pacific Northwest: Washington, Oregon;
West: Idaho, Montana, Wyoming, California, Nevada, Utah, Colorado;
Southwest: Arizona, New Mexico, Texas, Oklahoma;
Great Plains: North Dakota, South Dakota, Nebraska, Kansas;
Midwest: Minnesota, Iowa, Missouri, Wisconsin, Illinois, Michigan, Indiana, Ohio;
South: Arkansas, Louisiana, Kentucky, Tennessee, Mississippi, Alabama, Georgia, Florida,
      West Virginia, Virginia, North Carolina, South Carolina;
Mid-Atlantic: New York, Pennsylvania, New Jersey, Maryland, Delaware;
New England: Vermont, New Hampshire, Maine, Massachusetts, Connecticut, Rhode Island

How to Play!

Discuss regions of the United States. Determine in what region your state is located. Teacher or students call out names of other states; other students tell in what region that state is located.

 CHALLENGE: Name cities; others must identify the region.

WHAT TIME IS IT?

■ **PARTICIPATION:** Class

■ **MATERIALS:** map or globe where time zones are shown

How to Play!

Ask: If it is ____ o'clock here, what time is it in _____ (name a city)?

★ FAMOUS WORDS

■ **PARTICIPATION:** Class

■ **MATERIALS:** text of the Declaration of Independence, the preamble to the Constitution, the Gettysburg address, the Emancipation Proclamation, the engraving on the Statue of Liberty

How to Play!

Read the text. Discuss the power of speech.

WHERE DO YOU LIVE?

■ PARTICIPATION: Class

■ MATERIALS: paper and pencil

How to Play!

Make a list of various types of housing throughout the world and in different cultures. How are they alike? How are they different? Consider: Weather, natural resources, uses, and culture.

JUST A KID

■ PARTICIPATION: Class

How to Play!

Discuss: Did children grow up faster in the past? Relate to any historical periods you are now studying. Bring up boy soldiers, child labor, marriage age laws, and life expectancy.

★ WHAT DID THEY WEAR?

■ PARTICIPATION: Class

■ MATERIALS: a book on costumes of the time you are studying or a general reference book on costumes

How to Play!

Show a picture of the typical clothing of the time. Discuss comfort and utility. Be sure to note differences in the dress of different classes of people.

 CHALLENGE: Come up with a complete outfit for someone your age at that time in history.

THE ORIGINAL AMERICANS

■ PARTICIPATION: Class

■ MATERIALS: large sheet of paper and marker

How to Play!

As a class, make a list of as many Native American tribes as you can name. With research, add more each day.

 CHALLENGE: After the name of the tribe, write the area or region (e.g., Plains, Southwest).

★ GO WEST, YOUNG PERSON

■ PARTICIPATION: Class

■ MATERIALS: large sheet of paper and marker

How to Play!

Ask: If you were getting ready to go west in the mid-1800s, what would you take for the trip? Make a list.

CHALLENGE: What would you need when you are arrived at your destination?

IT GOES

■ PARTICIPATION: Class

■ MATERIALS: large sheet of paper and marker

How to Play!

Make a list of all forms of transportation.

IT'S YOUR DUTY

■ PARTICIPATION: Class

How to Play!

Make a list of the duties of a good citizen (adult).

SOLUTION ON PAGE 137.

NOW AND THEN

■ PARTICIPATION: Class

How to Play!

Consider the years or era being studied in history. Compare what was used at that time for what we use now: Microwave oven, disposable diapers, soap, air conditioning, mall, plastic bags, wristwatch, grocery store, electric light, car, suitcase, television news show, and paperback book.

PICK A CITY, ANY CITY

■ **PARTICIPATION:** Class/Partners

■ **MATERIALS:** atlas

How to Play!

One person opens to the index and randomly points to any city; others locate it on the map.

 CHALLENGE: Use longitude and latitude coordinates to find a place on the map.

★ ANSWER THE QUESTION

■ **PARTICIPATION:** Class/Partners

■ **MATERIALS:** paper and pencil, if needed

How to Play!

Select an event in history that you are studying. Pretend you could ask a question of one of the event's participants. Have another student guess what would be answered.

 CHALLENGE: What would they ask you?

WHO IS IT?

■ **PARTICIPATION:** Class/Partners

■ **MATERIALS:** paper and pencil

How to Play!

Have students write five clues about a person, place, or thing being studied in history. Make Clue 1 the hardest and Clue 5 the easiest. Partners or other members of the class must guess after each clue.

BRAVO!

■ **PARTICIPATION:** Class/Partners/Individuals

How to Play!

Act out a scene from any event you are studying.

★ WHAT'S IN THE NAME?

- ■ **PARTICIPATION:** Class/Partners/Individuals
- ■ **MATERIALS:** map or atlas

How to Play!

Search the atlas index for funny or strange names of cities in your state. Locate on a map.

 CHALLENGE: Do the same for other states. For an additional challenge, find out how a city got its name.

COME TO . . .

- ■ **PARTICIPATION:** Class/Partners/Individuals
- ■ **MATERIALS:** paper and pencil

How to Play!

Pick a country being studied. Have the students write a one- or two-line promo as if they were in charge of tourism advertising.

 CHALLENGE: Draw a picture to go with the promo using fancy lettering and color.

★ TIME MACHINE

- ■ **PARTICIPATION:** Class/Individuals

How to Play!

Tell the students: Imagine time travel has been perfected. In what one time or place would you like to travel?

CHALLENGE: What setting or year would be on your machine?

NAME THAT PLACE

- **PARTICIPATION:** Class/Individuals
- **MATERIALS:** map, newspapers, and news magazines

How to Play!

Have students bring in newspaper articles featuring a story about a foreign country. Mark that country on the map. See how many countries can be found.

A SPECIAL MEETING

- **PARTICIPATION:** Class/Individuals

How to Play!

Have the students imagine having a meeting with a major leader in the time you are studying. Ask: What would you say? What would that person say to you? Keep it simple; ask one or two questions about events at that time or get the leader's reaction to modern events.

YOU BE THE CURATOR

- **PARTICIPATION:** Class/Individuals
- **MATERIALS:** paper and pencil, if needed

How to Play!

Select one aspect of the era in history that you are studying. Have the students set up an imaginary exhibit where any artifact is available to you and money is no object. (Ideas: Food, medicine, battles/military, trade, communications, transportation, religion, science/inventions, politics, class differences, children, arts). Discuss or write briefly about your exhibit.

★ YOU'RE THE REPORTER

- **PARTICIPATION:** Partners
- **MATERIALS:** paper and pencil

How to Play!

One person interviews the other who is portraying a famous person in history.

★ HOW WILL IT BE?

- ■ PARTICIPATION: Partners
- ■ MATERIALS: paper and pencil

How to Play!

Conduct an "interview" with someone from the future.

HERE AND THERE

- ■ PARTICIPATION: Partners
- ■ MATERIALS: paper and pencil

How to Play!

One person pretends to be from another country (a country you are studying now). The other person questions him or her about that country.

DO YOU KNOW ALL 50?

- ■ PARTICIPATION: Individuals
- ■ MATERIALS: for each student, a map of the United States with states outlined

How to Play!

On the map, write the names of the states in their proper place.

? CHALLENGE: Write the names of the capitals in the correct states. For an additional challenge, indicate the location of the capital by a dot or star.

PARTY TIME

- ■ PARTICIPATION: Individuals
- ■ MATERIALS: paper and pencil

How to Play!

Tell the students: You are giving a party for six people. They must be historical figures or famous people. You want a good mix for interesting conversation. Whom do you invite? List the names. Post them on the bulletin board to display and discuss.

PRIVATE THOUGHTS

■ PARTICIPATION: Individuals

How to Play!

Keep a diary as if you were alive during the particular time period you are studying.

THE FOUR LARGEST

How to Play!

In the puzzle below, cross off these letters: B E G H J K M O Q S U V W X Y Z. The letters that are left on each line will spell a word when they are unscrambled.

G M F A C V I C I P

H Z K E O B Y J S M

T A T I A Z L X N C

W N A B N Q I D I K

V U B J Y S G O W E

C Q R I H X C T U A

I. _____ 2. _____ 3. _____ 4. _____

What are they? _____

SOLUTION ON PAGE 137.

TAKE A TRIP THROUGH CENTRAL AMERICA

How to Play!

Begin at the arrow. Connect the letters that spell out the names of the countries of Central America listed below. They are not all in one line! They may be right next to each other, above or below, or diagonal.

```
D  Z  E  L  B  D  T  E  C  J  D  K
I  N  W  G  E  A  B  J  M  S  A  E
F  L  M  R  U  Y  T  A  N  A  L  L
A  E  G  I  O  L  F  V  M  I  S  O
B  S  T  R  E  D  A  U  L  A  G  P
M  N  V  H  C  O  N  O  S  H  S  T
D  A  O  D  R  A  H  A  B  O  W  A
U  E  P  A  R  G  U  I  C  A  R  C
B  R  V  C  J  L  A  N  Y  U  I  P
A  O  I  R  K  M  T  A  A  C  G  H
S  N  F  C  A  R  Y  E  P  R  T  U
```

HONDURAS
COSTA RICA
BELIZE
EL SALVADOR
PANAMA
GUATEMALA
NICARAGUA

SOLUTION ON PAGE 137.

EXPLORE SOUTH AMERICA

In the puzzle below, circle the letters that spell the names of the countries of South America listed on page 35. When you are finished, the remaining letters will reveal an interesting fact.

```
      P U N T L A A
      R Y E N A I L O C
  A T A L E U Z E N E V
  E D U O N T A H E S U O U T
  H E G R N T R S U R I N A M E
  I P A A O F B M U A I N L A N
  D F R E N C H G U I A N A C
  H A I L A U E I E L I H C
      P S T A Y H E C S O U
      T Y R H U E U R N C
      M G O S G A T O
      P E R U C D L
      N I T Y O I
      T N T M R
      I A B H
      N I E W
      A V O
      R I L
        L
        O
        B
        D
```

PERU   BOLIVIA   PARAGUAY

CHILE   ECUADOR   SURINAME

BRAZIL   URUGUAY   ARGENTINA

GUYANA COLOMBIA   VENEZUELA

                          FRENCH GUIANA

_ _ _ _ _   _ _ _ _ _ ,   _ _ _ _ _ _ _ _

_ _   _ _ _   _ _ _ _ _ _ _ _ _ _   _ _ _ _

_ _ _ _ _ _ _ _ _ _ _ _ _ _ _ _ ,   _ _

_ _ _ _ _ _ _ _ _ _ _ _ _ _ _

_ _ _ _ _ _ _ _ _ _ _ _ .

SOLUTION ON PAGE 138.

CATEGORIES

How to Play!

Fill in the chart below with the names of continents, countries, and cities that begin with the letters that are down the left side of the paper. See how many you can name!

	CONTINENTS	COUNTRIES	CITIES
A			
E			
S			
N			

SOLUTION ON PAGE 139.

KWANZAA

How to Play!

The candle puzzle below contains the African words that are listed in capitals. When all letters are circled, the letters that are left will spell out what Kwanzaa celebrates.

WORD	TRANSLATION
UMOJA	unity
KUJICHAGULIA	self-determination
UJIMA	collective work and responsibility
UJAMAA	cooperative economics
NIA	purpose
KUUMBA	creativity
IMANI	faith

```
      A K F
    U R U I C
    J J J A N
    A N I A C
    M U C M I
    A L H N A
    A U A T B
    U M G R M
    I O U E U
    A J L N U
    D A I P K
    R I A D E
```

__ __ __ __ __ __   __ __ __ __ __ __

__ __ __   __ __ __ __ __

SOLUTION ON PAGE 139.

CANADA AND ITS CAPITALS

How to Play!

Fill in the puzzle boxes with the names of the provinces and territories of Canada, using the clues below, which are the capitals.

DOWN:
1. St. John's
2. Charlottetown
3. Toronto
5. Regina
6. Victoria
7. Halifax

ACROSS:
4. Fredericton
8. Yellowknife
9. Edmonton
10. Quebec City
11. Winnipeg
12. Whitehorse

WHITEHORSE!

SOLUTION ON PAGE 140.

LEIF ERIKSON THE EXPLORER

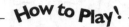

How to Play!

The words in all capital letters are hidden in the puzzle below. Find and circle them across, down, or diagonally.

LEIF Erikson was born in ICELAND. His father was ERIK the RED of NORWAY and his mother was THJODHILD. In 986, the family moved to GREENLAND. About the year 1000, Leif sailed to the coast of North AMERICA. Leif's brothers THORVALD and THORSTEIN and his sister FREYDIS were also explorers. Some books about the family's VOYAGES were The Greenlanders' SAGA and Erik the Red's Saga. Leif, often called Leif the LUCKY, sailed in a KNARR, which is an open BOAT. He and his crew traveled to Baffin Island, which they named Helluland (it means FLATSTONE Land). They also explored Labrador, called Markland (which means WOOD Land). Then they went on to what they named VINLAND (Wine Land), which is known in modern times as NEWFOUNDLAND. The Vikings called the Native Americans they found there by the NORSE name SKRAELINGS.

```
W  N  V  O  Y  A  G  E  S  R  O  N  A
B  O  A  T  G  K  R  P  G  E  R  E  S
T  H  O  R  S  T  E  I  N  W  R  C  V
E  V  B  D  A  M  E  R  I  C  A  I  Y
N  E  W  F  O  U  N  D  L  A  N  D  K
O  O  D  H  B  J  L  O  E  L  K  S  I
T  M  R  S  R  F  A  L  A  M  G  R  C
S  J  A  W  U  E  N  N  R  N  D  L  E
T  G  I  K  A  H  D  Y  K  C  U  L  L
A  C  F  R  E  Y  D  I  S  I  E  T  A
L  A  G  D  L  A  V  R  O  H  T  F  N
F  I  E  L  T  H  J  O  D  H  I  L  D
```

SOLUTION ON PAGE 140.

THE AGE OF EXPLORATION

How to Play!

Many adventurers made voyages of exploration in the 15th, 16th, and 17th centuries. In the puzzle below, track the explorer with a line drawn from his home square to the land or water he explored. He will travel north, south, east, or west. When moving, do not count the square where you are located.

		Madagascar and sea route to India	St. Lawrence River		
Bartolomeu Diaz	2E then 3S	Guiana		4S then 2W	Robert de La Salle
Vasco Nunez de Balboa	4S then 2E	around the globe	Philippines	2W 5S 1E	Hernando de Soto
Walter Raleigh	2E 2N 1W	North America		2W then 3N	Vasco da Gama
Francis Drake	2S 1E 4N		Cape of Good Hope	3S 1W 2N	Pedro Cabral
Samuel de Champlain	2E 2S 1W	Mississippi River to Louisiana	Brazil	2N 2W	John Cabot
Jacques Cartier	2E 6N		Pacific Ocean	1W 4N	Ferdinand Magellan
		Great Lakes	reaches Mississippi River		

SOLUTION ON PAGE 141.

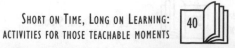

★ THANKSGIVING MATCH-UP

How to Play!

Match each item in Column 1 with a word or phrase in Column 2.

COLUMN 1

Pilgrims set sail from England

Pilgrims land in Massachusetts

Pilgrims and Native Americans
   first celebrate Thanksgiving

Oldest American holiday

Pilgrim's ship

First president to declare a day of thanks

English celebration at end of growing season

Lydia Maria Child wrote this poem

Cornucopia

Sarah Josepha Hale wrote to this president
   asking for a national Thanksgiving Day

Canadian Thanksgiving

United States Thanksgiving

COLUMN 2

George Washington

Fourth Thursday in November

"Over the River and Through the Wood"

September 1620

Horn of plenty

Fall, 1621

Mayflower

Second Monday in October

Thanksgiving

December 1620

Harvest Home

Abraham Lincoln

SOLUTION ON PAGE 142.

OCCUPATIONS

How to Play!

Hidden below are the names of some occupations. They may be across, down, backward, forward, or diagonal. After you have circled all of them, the remaining letters will spell out a message for you.

CHEF	PILOT	CASHIER	DESIGNER	ACCOUNTANT
ACTOR	BANKER	CHEMIST	MUSICIAN	PHARMACIST
GUARD	FARMER	JEWELER	ASTRONAUT	WOODWORKER
JUDGE	WELDER	PRINTER	DETECTIVE	INTERPRETER
NURSE	BUILDER	TEACHER	LIBRARIAN	VETERINARIAN

```
W  I  A  C  C  O  U  N  T  A  N  T  T
R  E  N  G  I  S  E  D  N  T  A  S  R
H  E  L  F  U  R  C  T  O  L  I  P  E
D  T  U  D  O  H  L  R  E  C  C  B  T
E  V  E  T  E  R  I  N  A  R  I  A  N
T  W  C  M  T  R  B  M  H  N  S  N  I
E  A  I  A  F  U  R  U  T  T  U  K  R
C  S  D  O  R  A  A  E  I  Y  M  E  P
T  E  A  C  H  E  R  N  O  L  U  R  G
I  S  G  P  T  P  I  M  O  F  D  U  H
V  R  I  D  R  N  A  H  E  R  A  E  K
E  U  Y  E  U  O  N  H  S  R  T  U  R
R  N  T  C  A  J  C  R  D  A  E  S  E
J  E  W  E  L  E  R  R  W  I  C  L  A
R  E  K  R  O  W  D  O  O  W  L  B  E
```

__ __ __ __ __ __ __ __ __ __ __ __ __ __, __ __ __ __

__ __ __ __ __ __ __ __ __ __ __ __ __ __

__ __ __ __ __ __ __ __ __ __ __ __ __ ?

SOLUTION ON PAGE 142.

ELECTIONS

How to Play!

Find the words in the list below in the puzzle. When you have circled all the words, the letters that are left will spell out a message.

```
S  T  O  L  L  A  B  V  O  S  R  T  T
E  T  U  R  N  O  U  T  E  E  E  I  N
U  N  E  G  O  A  P  T  T  K  G  O  G
S  L  A  T  E  L  A  U  C  C  I  I  I
S  L  H  V  A  D  R  I  I  T  S  H  A
I  O  C  N  I  N  T  P  A  D  T  C  P
C  P  K  D  S  U  I  G  M  T  R  E  M
A  Y  N  V  O  T  E  M  A  U  A  E  A
U  A  N  D  P  L  R  I  O  V  T  P  C
C  O  N  V  E  N  T  I  O  N  I  S  I
U  L  U  D  E  P  L  A  T  F  O  R  M
S  G  R  E  E  D  I  L  S  D  N  A  L
```

RUN	SLATE	ISSUES	CAMPAIGN	CANDIDATES
POLL	STUMP	TICKET	NOMINATE	CONVENTION
VOTE	BALLOT	RETURNS	PLATFORM	DELEGATION
BOOTH	CAUCUS	TURNOUT	LANDSLIDE	REGISTRATION
PLANK	SPEECH			

Message:

___ ___ ___ ___ ___ ___ ___ ___ ___ ___ ___ ___

___ ___ ___ ___ ___ ___ ___ ___ ___ ___ ___ ___ ___

SOLUTION ON PAGE 143.

CHAPTER 3

WEATHER—THE BIG PICTURE

- **PARTICIPATION:** Class
- **MATERIALS:** current newspapers with national or international weather maps
- **ADVANCE PREPARATION:** cut out the maps and label with the date

How to Play!

Have students chart the progress of fronts and storms across the country or continents.

CLEAR OR CLOUDY

- **PARTICIPATION:** Class
- **MATERIALS:** you may wish to have some almanacs available

How to Play!

Discuss typical weather in your state or region for each month or season. On the board, list what you have discussed.

CHALLENGE: Compare with other states or regions.

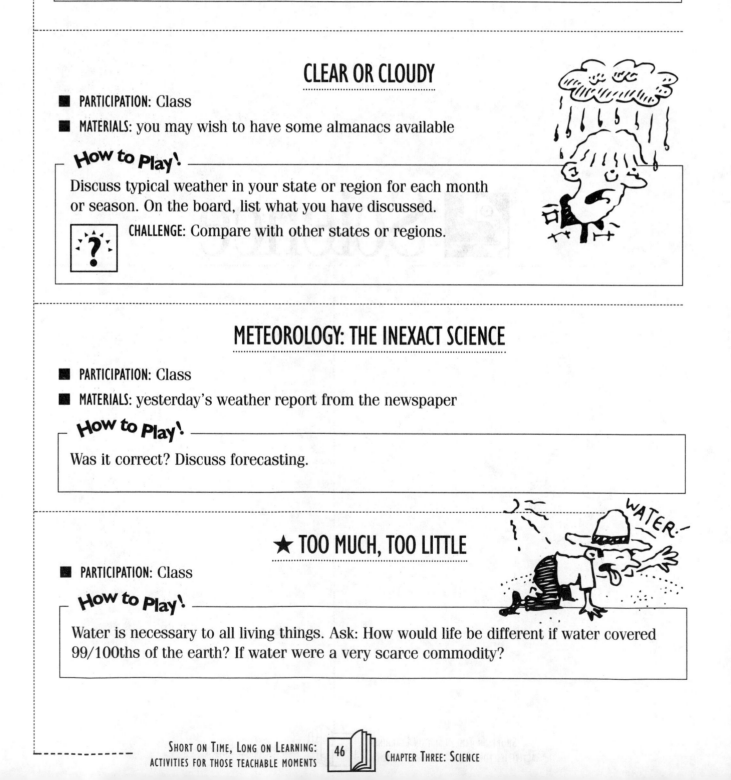

METEOROLOGY: THE INEXACT SCIENCE

- **PARTICIPATION:** Class
- **MATERIALS:** yesterday's weather report from the newspaper

How to Play!

Was it correct? Discuss forecasting.

★ TOO MUCH, TOO LITTLE

- **PARTICIPATION:** Class

How to Play!

Water is necessary to all living things. Ask: How would life be different if water covered 99/100ths of the earth? If water were a very scarce commodity?

★ IN THE NIGHT SKY

■ **PARTICIPATION:** Class

■ **MATERIALS:** a book about constellations

How to Play!

Find the picture of a constellation that will be in the sky in your hemisphere during this season. Have students look for it that night.

ONE AFTER ANOTHER

■ **PARTICIPATION:** Class/Partners/Individuals

■ **MATERIALS:** paper and pencil

How to Play!

Ask students to draw a food chain on the board or on paper, using animals you are now studying.

DESIGN IT YOURSELF

■ **PARTICIPATION:** Class/Partners/Individuals

■ **MATERIALS:** paper and pencil or markers

How to Play!

Have the students design a new zoo or wildlife habitat.

KNOWING THE NUMBERS

■ **PARTICIPATION:** Class

■ **MATERIALS:** labels from food boxes, jars, or bags that include the ingredients and nutrition labeling

How to Play!

Have a student read the ingredients from a label. Talk about the order that the ingredients are in and for what they may be used. Have students look at the nutrition labeling and try to guess which ingredients contribute to the fat and sodium content.

CHALLENGE: Compare two similar products, for example, cookies and crackers, pretzels and corn chips, two different cereals, and canned beans and canned corn.

THIS BONE'S CONNECTED TO THE . . .

■ **PARTICIPATION:** Class

■ **MATERIALS:** pictures or diagrams of the human body with bones, muscles, organs, and systems identified

How to Play!

Student or teacher points to a particular bone, muscle, organ, or system. Others must identify.

IT DOESN'T GROW IN A GROCERY STORE

■ **PARTICIPATION:** Class

■ **MATERIALS:** pictures of products or the products themselves, such as a leather purse, piece of paper, gum, banana, peanut, skein of yarn (with label), cotton shirt, or pair of pants.

How to Play!

Display the object or picture. Ask students what living things these products came from.

CHALLENGE: List as many products as you can from one source, for example, a tree.

SOMETHING DIFFERENT

- **PARTICIPATION:** Class
- **MATERIALS:** paper and pencil or markers

How to Play!

Lead students in a discussion of hybrids, genetic engineering, and improvements over the old fruits, vegetables, and other plants. If you could change some type of food that grows from plants, what would it be? What changes would you make? Draw a picture of the new food.

GOING TO THE STORE

- **PARTICIPATION:** Class/Partners/Individuals
- **MATERIALS:** paper and pencil

How to Play!

Have students make up a grocery list for a healthy meal.

CHALLENGE: Make up the list for a whole day's worth of meals and snacks.

GOOD FOOD

- **PARTICIPATION:** Class/Partners/Individuals
- **MATERIALS:** a picture of the food pyramid

How to Play!

Instruct students to plan a quick snack, keeping in mind the food pyramid.

FOOD FOR THOUGHT

...ICE CREAM, COOKIES, ROOT BEER...

- **PARTICIPATION:** Class/Individuals
- **MATERIALS:** paper and pencil

How to Play!

Tell students to think of the Perfect Meal with all the things they love to eat; then a healthy meal. Write them down.

★ INTRODUCING...

■ **PARTICIPATION:** Class

■ **MATERIALS:** books with short biographies of scientists. Some sources to use:

Scientists Who Changed the World by Philip Wilkinson and Michael Pollard (Chelsea House, 1994),

The Usborne Book of Scientists by Struan Reid and Patricia Fara (Usborne, 1992),

Inventors and Their Discoveries by Richard Kozar (Chelsea House, 1999),

African-American Scientists, *Hispanic Scientists*, *Native American Scientists*, all three by Jetty St. John (Capstone, 1996)

Ask your librarian for additional suggestions.

How to Play!

Read a short biography of a scientist to the class. If time allows, discuss the scientist's work, difficulties, and future uses of his or her discoveries or inventions.

READ ALL ABOUT IT

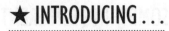

■ **PARTICIPATION:** Class/Individuals

■ **MATERIALS:** articles about science from the newspaper or magazines

■ **ADVANCE PREPARATION:** Instruct students to bring in any articles about science that they see in the local newspaper or from news magazines.

How to Play!

Read and post.

SOMETHING NEW

■ **PARTICIPATION:** Class

■ **MATERIALS:** long piece of paper, marker

■ **ADVANCE PREPARATION:** tape the paper to the wall and draw a time line on it (just decades until the 1800s, then years from 1800 on)

How to Play!

Discuss or read about one invention each day. Write it on the time line.

A HEALTHY CAREER

■ PARTICIPATION: Class

How to Play!

As a class, make a list of health professions. If time permits, discuss job responsibilities and/or education required.

YOU BE THE ARCHAEOLOGIST

■ PARTICIPATION: Class/Partners

■ MATERIALS: paper and pencil

How to Play!

Make a list of what archaeologists look for or find as clues

 CHALLENGE: Imagine that you are an archaeologist who discovered not just artifacts and bones, but a living, breathing person from 5,000 years ago. What would you ask him or her?

OVER AND OVER

■ PARTICIPATION: Class/Partners/Individuals

■ MATERIALS: paper and pencil

How to Play!

Think of patterns in nature—snowflakes, sand dunes, tree shapes, and so on. Make a list of as many patterns as you can. For each consider: What is alike? What is different?

★ ONE MAKES A DIFFERENCE

■ PARTICIPATION: Class/Individuals

How to Play!

Ask: What one thing can you do today to stop: Air pollution, water pollution, the landfill problem, and energy waste?

MORSE CODE

■ **PARTICIPATION:** Partners

■ **ADVANCE PREPARATION:** prepare a handout with Morse code or write it on the blackboard:

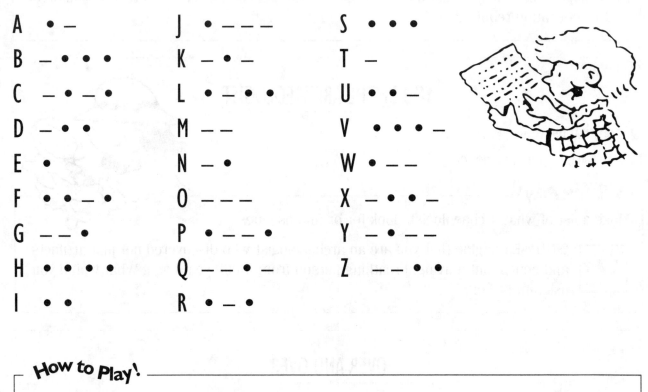

How to Play!

Have students make up messages using Morse code and then give them to their partners to solve.

OBSERVATION

■ **PARTICIPATION:** Partners/Individuals

■ **MATERIALS:** paper and pencil, magnifying glass (if needed)

How to Play!

Have students think of one thing in the classroom or outside it they can observe. It may be living or inanimate, large or small, or unique or one of many. Write observations to share with the class.

WEATHER WORDS

In each set of three words, one word does not belong. Circle that word. After you have circled the words, write down the letters that are underlined in those words, unscramble them, and you will have a word that relates to the puzzle.

blust<u>e</u>ry	wi<u>n</u>dy	cal<u>m</u>
<u>c</u>lear	clou<u>d</u>y	o<u>v</u>ercast
mil<u>d</u>	war<u>m</u>	fr<u>e</u>ezing
<u>h</u>ailing	ra<u>i</u>ning	sno<u>w</u>ing
ba<u>l</u>my	<u>c</u>hilly	<u>b</u>iting
f<u>a</u>ir	<u>s</u>moggy	f<u>o</u>ggy
swelt<u>e</u>ring	<u>h</u>umid	fros<u>t</u>y

SOLUTION ON PAGE 143.

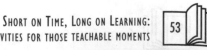

A STORMY PUZZLE

 How to Play!

Fill in the boxes with the stormy weather words.

CHALLENGE: Be able to tell what each is.

HAIL	SLEET	TEMPEST	DOWNPOUR
RAIN	SQUALL	TORNADO	HURRICANE
SNOW	CYCLONE	TYPHOON	CLOUDBURST
WIND	MONSOON	BLIZZARD	

SOLUTION ON PAGE 144.

OUT OF THIS WORLD

How to Play!

From the clue, decide what the word will be. Write it below, one letter in each space. When all the words are written, the letters in the boxes reading down will spell a word that relates to them all.

1. Milky Way is one
2. One body (such as moon or earth) blocks the light
3. Group of stars in a shape, usually with a name
4. Very hot ball of gases
5. Orbiting ball of ice
6. Explosion of a star
7. Orbiting rock
8. Small piece of rock that enters earth's atmosphere
9. Spiral galaxy that contains our solar system

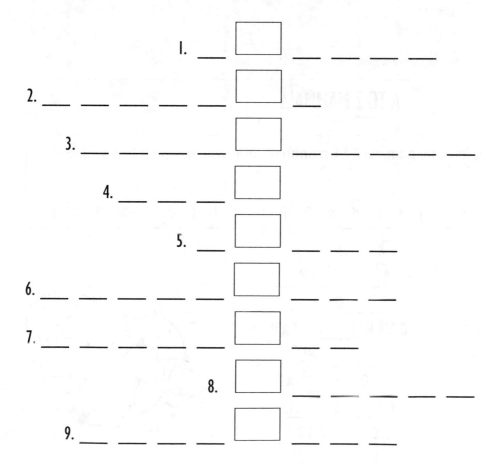

SOLUTION ON PAGE 144.

A PLANETARY QUIZ

How to Play!

Fill in the blank with the correct word about each planet.

Mercury   extreme _____, from 800 degrees F to -290 degrees F
Venus   is surrounded by clouds of _____ acid
Earth   _____ covers almost three-quarters of our planet
Mars   surface is a rocky _____
Jupiter   its Great Red Spot is a _____ cloud
Saturn   has _____ made of dust and ice
Uranus   15 _____ orbit this planet
Neptune   its moon, Triton, is the only one with a backward _____ (east to west)
Pluto   _____ planet of the solar system

storm	moons	temperatures
sulfuric	orbit	rings
water	smallest	desert

SOLUTION ON PAGE 144.

A TO Z MAMMALS

How to Play!

Fill in the blanks to complete the names of 11 mammals. You will use each letter of the alphabet once.

A B C D E F G H I J K L M N O P Q R S T U V W X Y Z

K ___ A ___ A
A A R ___ ___ A R ___
___ O ___
O R A N ___ ___ T A N
___ ___ M E L
___ O ___ ___ A T
G A ___ E L L ___
___ A C K ___ A B B I ___
L ___ ___ X
D O L ___ ___ I N
___ ___ U ___ R R E L

SOLUTION ON PAGE 145.

WHAT'S THE DIFFERENCE?

How to Play!

Birds and reptiles have some things in common. Other features are very different. In the circles below fill in the things they have in common where the circles meet. Write the other things about them in the rest of their circles.

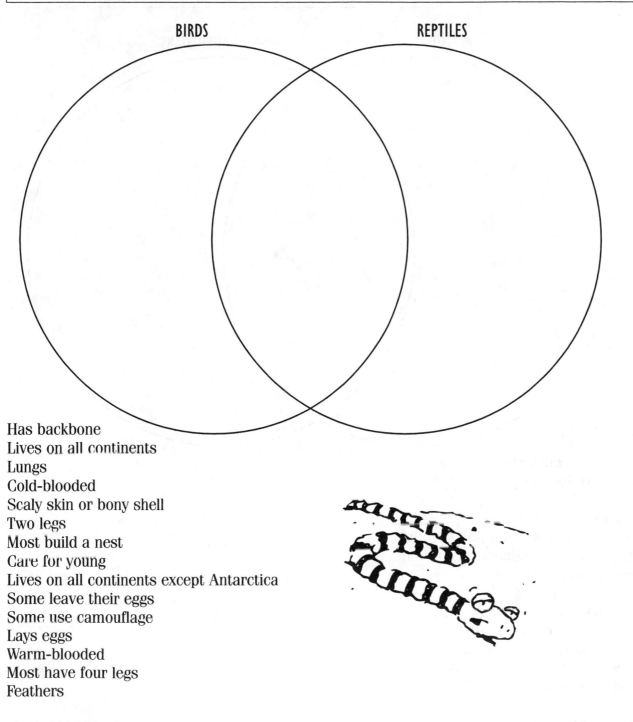

BIRDS   REPTILES

Has backbone
Lives on all continents
Lungs
Cold-blooded
Scaly skin or bony shell
Two legs
Most build a nest
Care for young
Lives on all continents except Antarctica
Some leave their eggs
Some use camouflage
Lays eggs
Warm-blooded
Most have four legs
Feathers

SOLUTION ON PAGE 145.

WHAT'S THE DIFFERENCE II?

How to Play!

On the list below, you will see some phrases that describe fish, others that describe amphibians, and others that may apply to both. Write the correct phrase in the circles. The phrases that are true for both fish and amphibians go in the middle where the circles overlap.

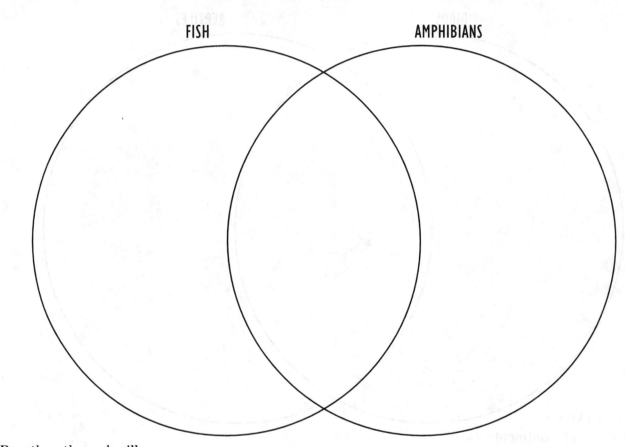

Breathes through gills
Most have four legs
Cold-blooded
Must live in water
Breathes through lungs and skin (adult)
Lives on every continent except Antarctica
Lays eggs in water
Has fins and tail
Has backbone
Many have sticky tongues
Can live in water and on land
Lives in every ocean, sea, lake, and river
Most have teeth

SOLUTION ON PAGE 145.

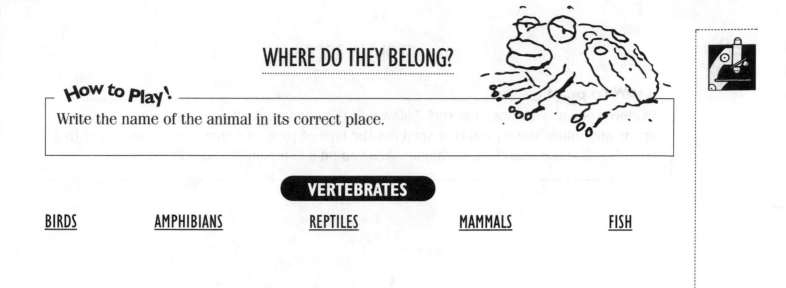

WHERE DO THEY BELONG?

How to Play!

Write the name of the animal in its correct place.

VERTEBRATES

BIRDS   AMPHIBIANS   REPTILES   MAMMALS   FISH

INVERTEBRATES

INSECTS   INVERTEBRATES, NOT INSECTS

newt	mole	penguin	flatworm	rhinoceros
ant	snake	shark	turkey	cockroach
clam	toad	sponge	whale	seahorse
eel	moth	frog	gecko	bumblebee
bat	dove	trout	squid	salamander
turtle	toucan	crocodile		

SOLUTION ON PAGE 146.

GEOLOGY ROCKS!

How to Play!

Explore your way through the rock below and the many rocks it contains. Start at each arrow and follow the letters that spell out the type of rock, and then four examples of that type. Do all three searches; each one takes you on a completely different path.

TYPES: Metamorphic, sedimentary, igneous

EXAMPLES: basalt, flint, gneiss, granite, gypsum, marble, obsidian, pumice, quartzite, sandstone, shale, slate

SOLUTION ON PAGE 146.

THE MANY KINDS OF ENERGY

How to Play!

See if you can find 12 types of energy using the code below. This is a kind of scrambled letter code that can be known by its password, which is written first, with the rest of the letters of the alphabet following. Look for the letter in the top line (the code line), then write the letter that appears below it.

Here's your code. Password: **W O R K**

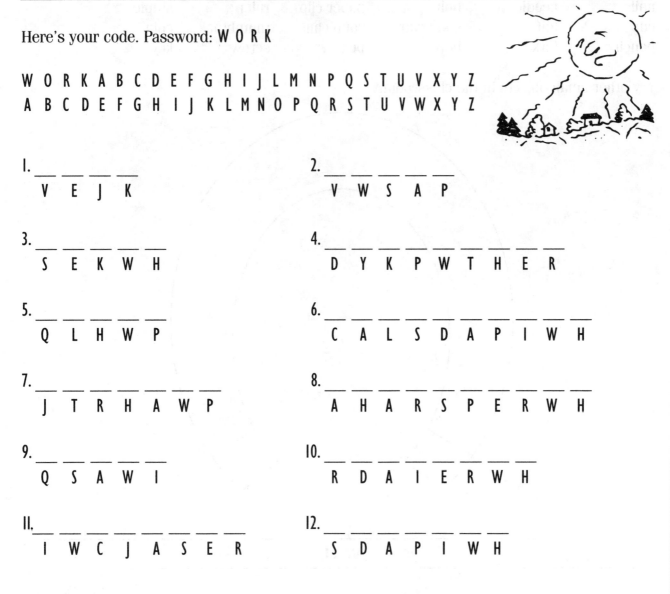

```
W O R K A B C D E F G H I J L M N P Q S T U V X Y Z
A B C D E F G H I J K L M N O P Q R S T U V W X Y Z
```

1. _ _ _ _
   V E J K

2. _ _ _ _ _
   V W S A P

3. _ _ _ _ _
   S E K W H

4. _ _ _ _ _ _ _ _ _
   D Y K P W T H E R

5. _ _ _ _ _
   Q L H W P

6. _ _ _ _ _ _ _ _ _ _
   C A L S D A P I W H

7. _ _ _ _ _ _
   J T R H A W P

8. _ _ _ _ _ _ _ _ _
   A H A R S P E R W H

9. _ _ _ _ _
   Q S A W I

10. _ _ _ _ _ _ _ _
    R D A I E R W H

11. _ _ _ _ _ _ _ _
    I W C J A S E R

12. _ _ _ _ _ _ _
    S D A P I W H

 CHALLENGE: See if you can make up a code with a different password and send secret messages to your friends!

SOLUTION ON PAGE 146.

MAGNETIC OR NOT?

nail	needle	bolt	paper clip	ruler	staple
cup	foil	soda can	soup can	thumbtack	coin
pencil	fork	book	pen	screw	key

Try other small objects in the classroom.

WALL

watch	videotape	chair	compass
jewelry	computer	tape recorder	computer disk
audiotape	light bulb	video recorder	television

SOLUTION ON PAGE 146.

THOSE TRAVELING SEEDS

CALIFORNIA, HERE I COME!

How to Play!

Unscramble the letters below to make words that are the carriers of seeds.

ruf _ _ _
        8

manslia _ _ _ _ _ _ _
             10

trawe _ _ _ _ _
            6

treheaw _ _ _ _ _ _ _
                 12 2

sltanp lesmevehts _ _ _ _ _   _ _ _ _ _ _ _ _ _
                      9   14   15

nwid _ _ _ _
         1

poplee _ _ _ _ _ _
              7   4

slecoht _ _ _ _ _ _ _
            11 5

shaftree _ _ _ _ _ _ _ _
                   13   3

When all letters have been unscrambled, transfer the letter over the number above to the corresponding blanks below. Using the clues, complete the word. All words are parts of plants. When the words are complete, you'll have a word in the boxes reading down.

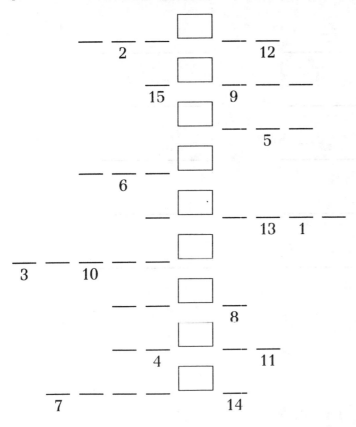

_ _ [ ] _ _   pollen is received here
  2   12

[ ]   leaf part that protects the flower
 15   9

[ ]   brings up water from underground
      5

[ ]   leaves and branches grow from here
 6

[ ]   the center of a flower
     13 1

[ ]   pollen is made here
3 10

[ ]   grows from the stem
    8

[ ]   the colorful part of a flower
 4   11

[ ]   powder that is transferred to stigma
 7   14

SOLUTION ON PAGE 147.

How to Play!

The matter is lumped together in a blob below. Sort it out so each item is listed as a solid, liquid, or gas.

milk   carbon monoxide   syrup   sand   sugar
ice   nitrogen   dust   helium   shampoo
steam   blood   minerals   ketchup   juice
sponge   carbon dioxide   glass   mercury   oxygen
oil   air   crystals

SOLID	LIQUID	GAS
_____	_____	_____
_____	_____	_____
_____	_____	_____
_____	_____	_____
_____	_____	_____
_____	_____	_____
_____	_____	

SOLUTION ON PAGE 147.

INSIDE THE CELL

How to Play!

Use the clues and the code to figure out the words below. When you are finished, use the code to answer the question.

CODE:

A	B	C	D	E	F	G	H	I	J	K	L	M	N	O	P	Q	R	S	T	U	V	W	X	Y	Z
12	1	18	6	8	3	17	5	16	19	7	21	14	4	20	24	9	10	22	23	2	11	25	13	26	15

1. Surrounds the entire cell

     __ __ __ __ __ __ __ __
     14 8 14 1 10 12 4 8

2. Substance that everything moves around in

     __ __ __ __ __ __ __ __ __
     18 26 23 20 24 21 12 22 14

3. Bits of nutrients are broken down for energy here

     __ __ __ __ __ __ __ __ __ __ __ __
     14 16 23 20 18 5 20 4 6 10 16 12

4. Makes protein

     __ __ __ __ __ __ __ __
     10 16 1 20 22 20 14 8

5. Helps out when cells divide

     __ __ __ __ __ __ __ __ __ __
     18 8 4 23 10 16 20 21 8 22

6. "Center" for everything cell does

     __ __ __ __ __ __ __
     4 2 18 21 8 2 22

7. Parts inside cells that have special jobs

     __ __ __ __ __ __ __ __ __ __
     20 10 17 12 4 8 21 21 8 22

Where were cells first seen?

__ __ __ __ __   __   __ __ __ __ __ __ __ __ __ __
2 4 6 8 10   12   14 16 18 10 20 22 18 20 24 8

SOLUTION ON PAGE 147.

CHAPTER 4

²⁄₄ Math

A REALLY BIG NUMBER

■ **PARTICIPATION:** Class

How to Play!

Write the numbers 1,000, 1 million, and 1 billion on the board. Then write a googol: a 1 with 100 zeros after it. Then explain a googolplex, a 1 with a googol zeros after it. For each number, have students think of objects for which there could be that number.

PART OF IT

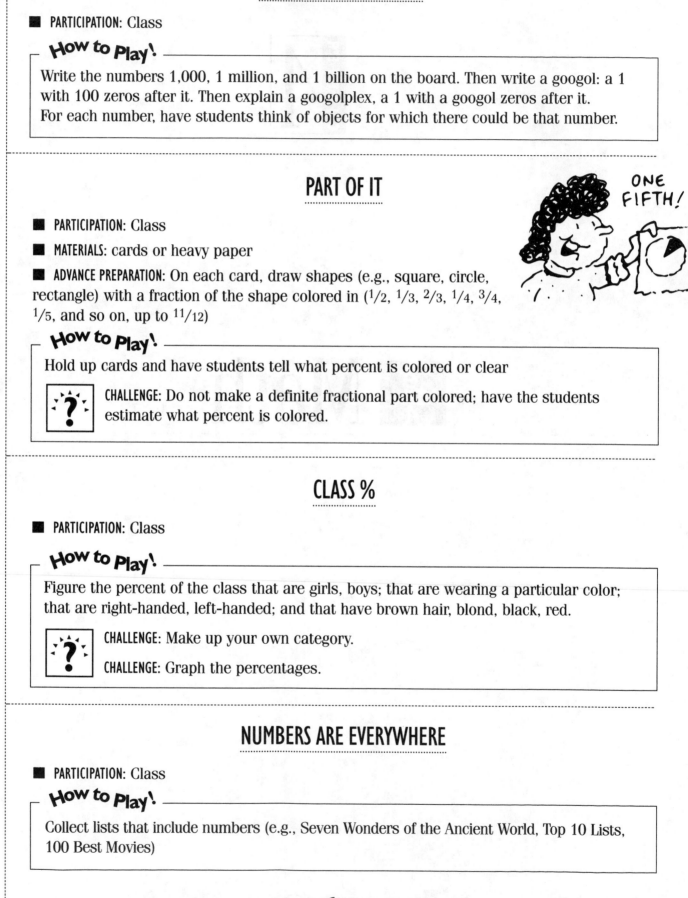

ONE FIFTH!

■ **PARTICIPATION:** Class

■ **MATERIALS:** cards or heavy paper

■ **ADVANCE PREPARATION:** On each card, draw shapes (e.g., square, circle, rectangle) with a fraction of the shape colored in ($1/2$, $1/3$, $2/3$, $1/4$, $3/4$, $1/5$, and so on, up to $11/12$)

How to Play!

Hold up cards and have students tell what percent is colored or clear

? **CHALLENGE:** Do not make a definite fractional part colored; have the students estimate what percent is colored.

CLASS %

■ **PARTICIPATION:** Class

How to Play!

Figure the percent of the class that are girls, boys; that are wearing a particular color; that are right-handed, left-handed; and that have brown hair, blond, black, red.

? **CHALLENGE:** Make up your own category.

CHALLENGE: Graph the percentages.

NUMBERS ARE EVERYWHERE

■ **PARTICIPATION:** Class

How to Play!

Collect lists that include numbers (e.g., Seven Wonders of the Ancient World, Top 10 Lists, 100 Best Movies)

I'M THINKING OF A NUMBER

■ PARTICIPATION: Class

How to Play!

One student thinks of a number and must tell the number of places in hundreds, tens, or ones. Others must guess, and the first student must tell them if their guess is high or low.

GETTING CLOSER

■ PARTICIPATION: Class

How to Play!

One student says a number, then calls on someone to round it off. (Determine ahead of time whether the number will be rounded off to the nearest ten, nearest hundred, and so on.)

★ ROUND OFF

■ PARTICIPATION: Class

■ MATERIALS: atlas or almanac

How to Play!

Look up the population of cities in your state. Round the number to the nearest 100; 1,000; or 10,000 (depending on size). Move on to other cities in the country.

THERE'S MORE THAN ONE WAY

■ PARTICIPATION: Class

How to Play!

Write a number on the board. Discuss: How many different ways can that number be portrayed? (e.g., Roman numerals, sign language, beads on an abacus, written, typed, money, base 12, and so on)

HOW LONG?

■ PARTICIPATION: Class

■ MATERIALS: stopwatch, paper, and pencil

How to Play!

Use the stopwatch to time the students as they perform a simple task, such as walking from one end of the room to the other, arranging books on their desk, and sorting small objects. Have students calculate the average time of the class.

A NEW ANGLE

■ PARTICIPATION: Class

How to Play!

Have one student draw an acute angle on the board. The rest of the class makes an acute angle, each student using their arm or leg with elbow or knee as the point. Do the same for a right angle and an obtuse angle.

PLANNING A PARTY

■ PARTICIPATION: Class

■ ADVANCE PREPARATION: Write on the board the following:
    ice cream bars, package of 12—$2.59
    cookies, package of 25—$1.99
    juice, box of eight containers—$4.39

How to Play!

Calculate how much the class will need to spend if buying these items for a party. Be sure to buy enough containers so everyone can have one of each. Add more items and prices if time allows.

WHAT TIME IS IT?

■ PARTICIPATION: Class

■ MATERIALS: globes or maps that show the Prime Meridian and time zones throughout the world

How to Play!

Have one student call out a time in a particular city. The others must tell what time it is in your locality.

DOLLARS AND PERCENTS

PARTICIPATION: Class/Partners

MATERIALS: paper and pencil, if needed

How to Play!

Teacher or one student calls out a percentage on a given amount of money (Example: "30 percent of $20"). Others must give the answer.

FROM MILLENNIUM TO MICRO-SECOND

PARTICIPATION: Class/Partners/Individuals

How to Play!

Make a list of time words. If time permits, put in order, largest to smallest.

WHICH IS IT?

PARTICIPATION: Class/Partners/Individuals

ADVANCE PREPARATION: On the board or on paper, write two numbers.

How to Play!

Call on someone to write a > or < sign between the numbers. Then, write two math facts using addition, subtraction, multiplication, or division; have a student write > or <.

CHALLENGE: Use increasingly complex math statements.

FOR SALE

PARTICIPATION: Class/Partners/Individuals

MATERIALS: classified ads section of the newspaper

How to Play!

Assign the class, group, or individual student an amount of money. Have them go through the For Sale section of the paper to see what is the best deal they could make. Decide ahead of time or as a group what they will buy (e.g., car, musical instrument, furniture).

★ REALLY, REALLY BIG

■ **PARTICIPATION:** Class/Partners/Individuals

■ **MATERIALS:** an almanac, atlas, *Guinness* book

How to Play!

Use the resources to look up fascinating facts that have to do with large numbers.

A MEAL OUT

■ **PARTICIPATION:** Class/Partners/Individuals

■ **MATERIALS:** paper and pencil

■ **ADVANCE PREPARATION:** Collect some menus from local restaurants.

How to Play!

Have the students select food, then figure their total with food ordered, tax, and tip.

AN ANGULAR TOWN

■ **PARTICIPATION:** Class/Partners/Individuals

■ **MATERIALS:** paper and pencil, if needed

How to Play!

On the board or on paper, have the students draw houses and buildings that (1) are composed of all right angles, (2) are composed of acute angles, and (3) are composed of obtuse angles.

PART OF IT

■ **PARTICIPATION:** Class/Individuals

■ **MATERIALS:** paper with a number of circles and squares preprinted on it

How to Play!

Name a fraction and have students divide the circle or square to show the fraction.

HOW MANY?

- **PARTICIPATION:** Class/Individuals
- **MATERIALS:** paper and pencil

How to Play!

Have each student or the class pick a very large number. Imagine what it would be like to have that number of any object. Write about it.

AN ECONOMICAL PIZZA

- **PARTICIPATION:** Class/Individuals
- **MATERIALS:** paper and pencil
- **ADVANCE PREPARATION:** Write on the board the following:

Pizza sauce	16 oz. $1.89	20 oz. $2.29
Cheese	8 oz. $2.46	12 oz. $3.11
Pizza crust mix	6 oz. 45¢	10 oz. 79¢

How to Play!

Have the students calculate the best buy for these products.

 CHALLENGE: Make up some coupons for the products (e.g., 20 cents off sauce). Does this change your answer?

QUICK THINKING

- **PARTICIPATION:** Partners

How to Play!

One student pretends that he is selling movie tickets. (Determine the price in dollars and cents, not just dollars.) Have the other student say how many tickets are needed. The seller must tell the buyer how much hc owes. Do the same with other items: Ice cream cones, doughnuts, popcorn, and other things a child might buy.

CHANGE, PLEASE

■ **PARTICIPATION:** Partners

■ **MATERIALS:** a variety of items (e.g., book, small toy, CD, jacket, shoes, various school supplies, stuffed animal), play money in dollar form and coins

■ **ADVANCE PREPARATION:** Label the items with prices.

How to Play!

Distribute the money to the students. Have half of them select an item and pay for it. Their partners must make change.

YOU HAVE A POINT

■ **PARTICIPATION:** Partners

■ **MATERIALS:** graph paper and pencil

How to Play!

On a sheet of graph paper, one student plots out points to make a picture. After establishing x-y coordinates, the student should then tell his partner the coordinates to draw the same picture on his paper.

HOW GOOD IS YOUR MEMORY?

■ **PARTICIPATION:** Partners

■ **MATERIALS:** paper and pencil

■ **ADVANCE PREPARATION:** Write a series of numbers on a piece of paper, beginning with a three-digit number and going up to a 10-digit number.

How to Play!

The student who wrote the numbers shows them, one at a time, to his partner. Then, that partner must repeat it back. Is there a limit to how many numbers we can remember?

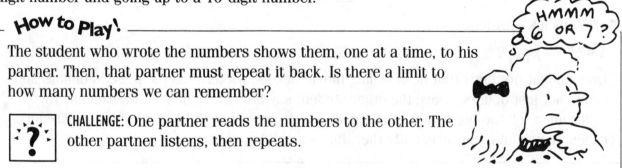

CHALLENGE: One partner reads the numbers to the other. The other partner listens, then repeats.

IT'S IN THE AREA

■ PARTICIPATION: Partners

■ MATERIALS: graph paper, scissors, paper, and pencil

How to Play!

Instruct the students to cut a shape from the graph paper (on the lines!), then give it to their partner who will figure out how many square units that shape represents. If you wish, determine as a class what the units should be (e.g., inches, feet, yards).

STACK IT UP

■ PARTICIPATION: Partners/Individuals

■ MATERIALS: blocks

How to Play!

Have groups or individuals use the blocks in different configurations to figure volume.

ADD IT UP

■ PARTICIPATION: Individuals

■ MATERIALS: an almanac or other source that lists world population

How to Play!

Tell the students you have a great idea that you want everyone in the world to know. If you tell one person now and that person tells two people the next minute; then, those two each tell two people the next minute; then, those four each tell two people the next minute, in effect doubling the number of people each minute, how long before all the people in the world will know?

ALL OF IT

■ PARTICIPATION: Individuals

■ MATERIALS: paper and pencil

How to Play!

Have students make a pie chart, showing "How I Spend My Day," "Where My Allowance Goes," or any other topic that is personally relevant to them.

HOW BIG?

■ **PARTICIPATION:** Individuals

■ **MATERIALS:** graph paper and pencil

How to Play!

Have students draw an outline of a room on graph paper. Determine ahead of time the length each square will represent. Determine the area of the room.

CHALLENGE: Draw a room that is L-shaped or some other shape that is not a square or rectangle.

WHAT TIME?

■ **PARTICIPATION:** Individuals

■ **ADVANCE PREPARATION:** On the board, write a series of times, such as:

If it is 2:45 and the trip takes 3 hours and 12 minutes, you will arrive at _____

If it is 9:01 and the trip takes 4 hours and 59 minutes, you will arrive at _____

If it is 10:37 and the trip takes 38 minutes, you will arrive at _____

If it is 5:10 a.m. and it takes 12 hours, 55 minutes, you will arrive at _____

How to Play!

Have the students complete each sentence.

SOLUTION ON PAGE 148.

NAME THAT SHAPE

How to Play!

Fill in the blanks below with the name of the shape. When you are finished, the boxes going down will spell out the word that is the study of these shapes.

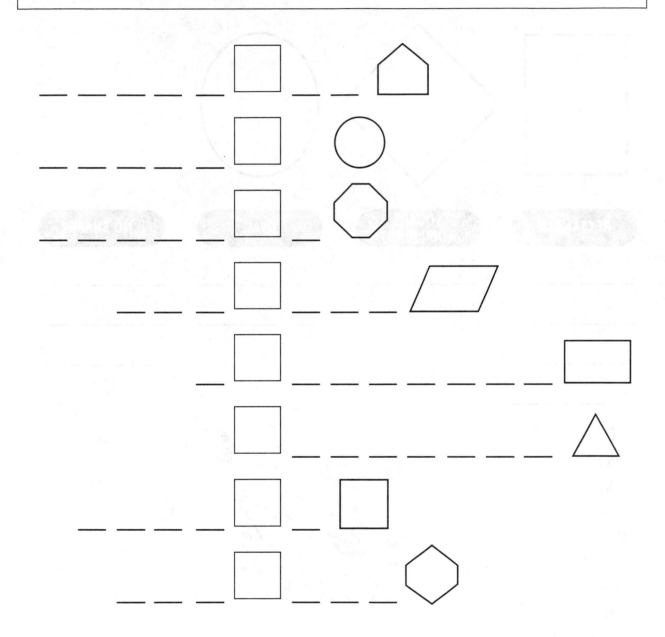

SOLUTION ON PAGE 148.

SPORT SHAPES

How to Play!

Below each shape, write the name of the sport that is played on that shape field or court.

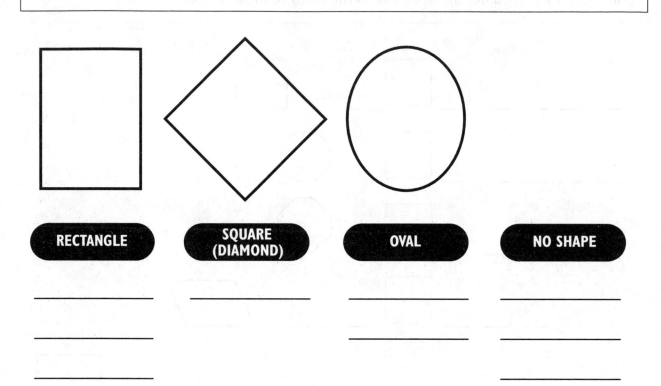

RECTANGLE	SQUARE (DIAMOND)	OVAL	NO SHAPE

Soccer
Track
Tennis
Golf
Baseball
Skiing
Football
Speed skating
Surfing
Basketball

SOLUTION ON PAGE 148.

ROMAN NUMERAL SIGNS

How to Play!

Below are signs that you might see on the highway, except that each has one or more Roman numerals on it. Below the sign, write the number that you would normally see.

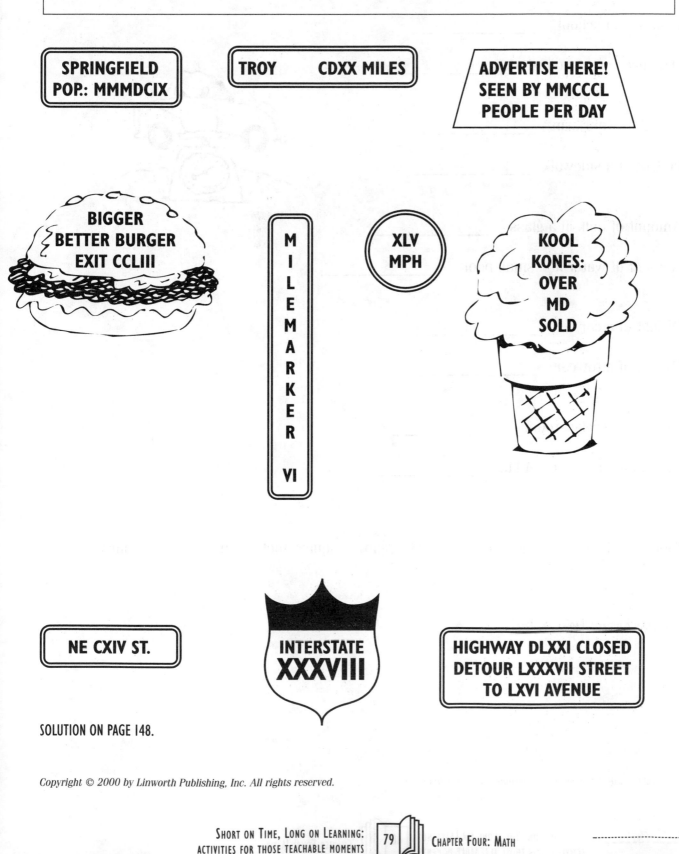

SPRINGFIELD POP.: MMMDCIX

TROY   CDXX MILES

ADVERTISE HERE! SEEN BY MMCCCL PEOPLE PER DAY

BIGGER BETTER BURGER EXIT CCLIII

MILE MARKER VI

XLV MPH

KOOL KONES: OVER MD SOLD

NE CXIV ST.

INTERSTATE XXXVIII

HIGHWAY DLXXI CLOSED DETOUR LXXXVII STREET TO LXVI AVENUE

SOLUTION ON PAGE 148.

HOW SHOULD I MEASURE?

How to Play!

Select the best unit for measuring the following: (You might use a word more than once!)

Distance to school _____

Distance across your desk _____

Length of your arm _____

Length of a sidewalk _____

Amount of milk in a glass _____

Amount of water in a small pool _____

Weight of a car _____

Weight of a toy car _____

Area of your classroom _____

Area of a large piece of land _____

foot   gallon   ounce   acre   yard   cup   square foot   mile   ton   inch

SOLUTION ON PAGE 149.

GOING UP, GOING DOWN

quart, tablespoon, gallon, cup, pint, teaspoon

kilometer, centimeter, meter, millimeter, decimeter

billion, quintillion, trillion, quadrillion, million

year, week, millennium, decade, day, fortnight, century, month

SOLUTION ON PAGE 149.

MEASURE THIS

How to Play!

Here are some unusual measures. Match the name with the amount and with something that it might measure.

MEASURE	AMOUNT	WHAT IT WILL MEASURE
score	12 dozen	salt
hand	13	years
gross	1 nautical mile per hour	doughnuts
pinch	500 pieces	horse's height
knot	20	ocean liner speed
ream	just a bit	pencils
baker's dozen	4 in.	paper

SOLUTION ON PAGE 149.

FOUR SCORE...

WHAT WILL COME NEXT?

How to Play!

On each spoke of the Ferris wheel, write the next numbers in the series. On the car at the end of the spoke, write the "rule" that each series follows.

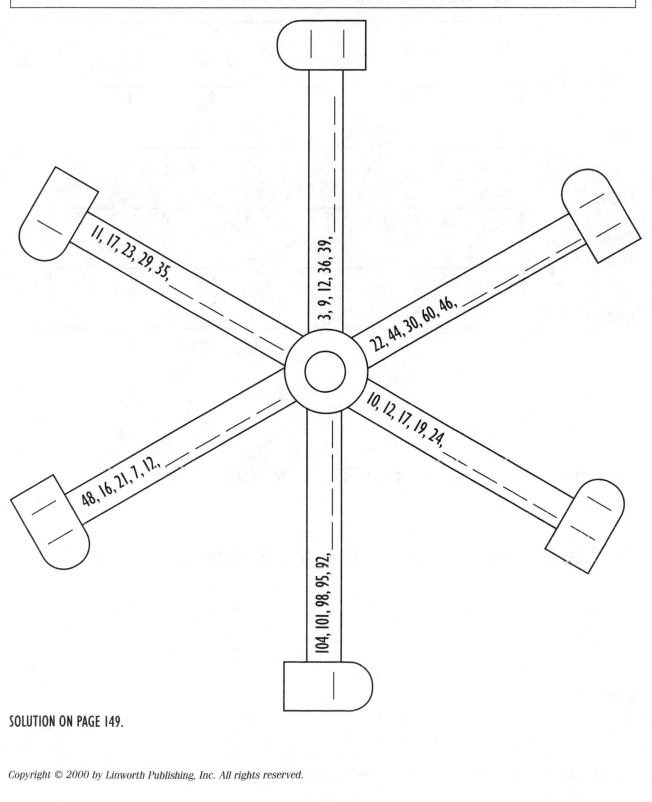

11, 17, 23, 29, 35, _____

3, 9, 12, 36, 39, _____

22, 44, 30, 60, 46, _____

48, 16, 21, 7, 12, _____

10, 12, 17, 19, 24, _____

104, 101, 98, 95, 92, _____

SOLUTION ON PAGE 149.

EXPANDED NUMBERS

How to Play!

Write each number below in its expanded form. After you have filled in all the blanks, transfer the letter that is under the number to the correct place below. There you will spell out a message about the fourth number.

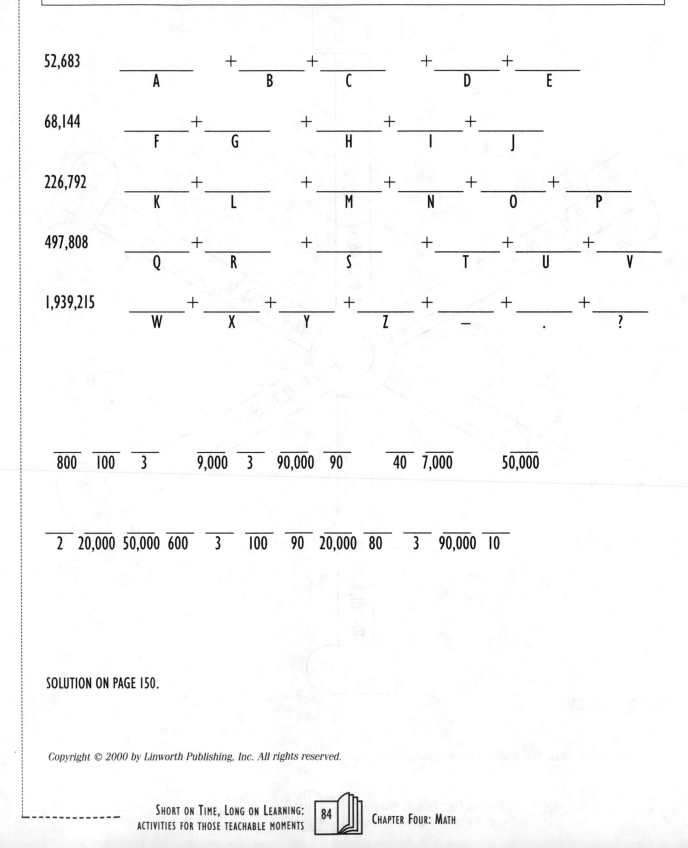

52,683   _____ + _____ + _____   _____ + _____
          A   B   C   D   E

68,144   _____ + _____   _____ + _____   _____ + _____
          F   G   H   I   J

226,792   _____ + _____   _____ + _____   _____ + _____   _____
          K   L   M   N   O   P

497,808   _____ + _____   _____ + _____   _____ + _____   _____ + _____
          Q   R   S   T   U   V

1,939,215 _____ + _____ + _____ + _____   _____ + _____   _____ + _____
          W   X   Y   Z   —   .   ?

_____ _____ _____   _____ _____ _____ _____   _____ _____   _____
 800   100   3   9,000   3   90,000   90   40   7,000   50,000

_____ _____ _____ _____   _____   _____   _____ _____ _____   _____ _____ _____
  2   20,000 50,000   600   3   100   90   20,000   80   3   90,000   10

SOLUTION ON PAGE 150.

HURRY UP!

What time will you need to leave in order to do the activities below?

If you must catch a bus at 8:05, and it takes you 7 minutes to walk to the bus stop, what time will you need to leave home? _____

Your dental appointment is at 4:15. Mom says it takes 35 minutes to drive to the dentist's office. What time must you leave? _____

If your soccer game starts at 7:30, and you need 2 minutes to walk to the field, what time must you leave your house? _____

You and your family are invited to grandmas at 12:30. If it takes 2 hours and 15 minutes to drive there, when will you need to leave? _____

Your flight is scheduled to take off at 1:23. You must leave home 1½ hours before that time to travel to the airport and check in. When must you leave home? _____

If you and your family are driving to a friend's home to arrive at noon, and the trip takes 18 hours, when would you need to start the drive? _____

SOLUTION ON PAGE 150.

A FRACTIONAL QUILT

How to Play!

Follow the directions below for each section of the quilt.

Color 3/4 of the vertical stripes yellow, 1/8 orange, and 1/8 red.
Put X's on 1/2 of the circles, a smiley face on 1/3, and outline 1/6.
Draw wavy lines on 1/6 of the squares, straight lines in 1/6, and zigzag lines in 2/3.
Next to 2/5 of the moons, draw a cloud, draw a star next to 1/10, and color 1/2 yellow.
Color 1/5 of the ovals green, 2/3 red, and 2/15 blue.
Color 2/3 of the flowers red, 2/9 pink, and 1/9 white.

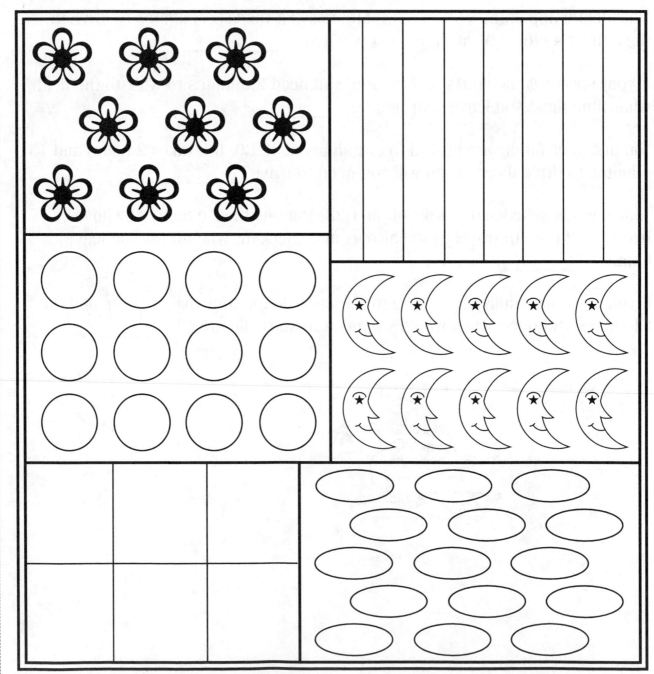

TIC-TAC-TOE

How to Play!

Draw a line through the three fractions or whole numbers that are equivalent.

$\frac{10}{2}$	$\frac{12}{2}$	$\frac{16}{4}$
$\frac{9}{3}$	**6**	$\frac{10}{3}$
$\frac{4}{2}$	$\frac{18}{3}$	$\frac{15}{5}$

3	$\frac{18}{9}$	$\frac{9}{3}$
$\frac{21}{3}$	$\frac{8}{4}$	$\frac{10}{4}$
$\frac{20}{5}$	$\frac{16}{4}$	$\frac{12}{3}$

$\frac{18}{4}$	$\frac{24}{12}$	$\frac{7}{2}$
$\frac{9}{2}$	$\frac{9}{8}$	$\frac{16}{4}$
$4\frac{1}{2}$	$\frac{8}{6}$	$\frac{24}{6}$

$\frac{30}{9}$	$\frac{8}{3}$	$\frac{45}{15}$
$\frac{18}{6}$	$\frac{10}{3}$	$\frac{27}{9}$
$\frac{30}{10}$	$\frac{36}{18}$	$3\frac{1}{3}$

$\frac{11}{4}$	$\frac{22}{8}$	$2\frac{3}{4}$
$\frac{12}{8}$	$\frac{34}{16}$	$\frac{6}{4}$
$\frac{9}{4}$	$\frac{36}{24}$	$\frac{24}{12}$

SOLUTION ON PAGE 150.

A WEB OF NUMBERS

How to Play!

In the spider web below, fill in the fraction, decimal, and percent in each section.

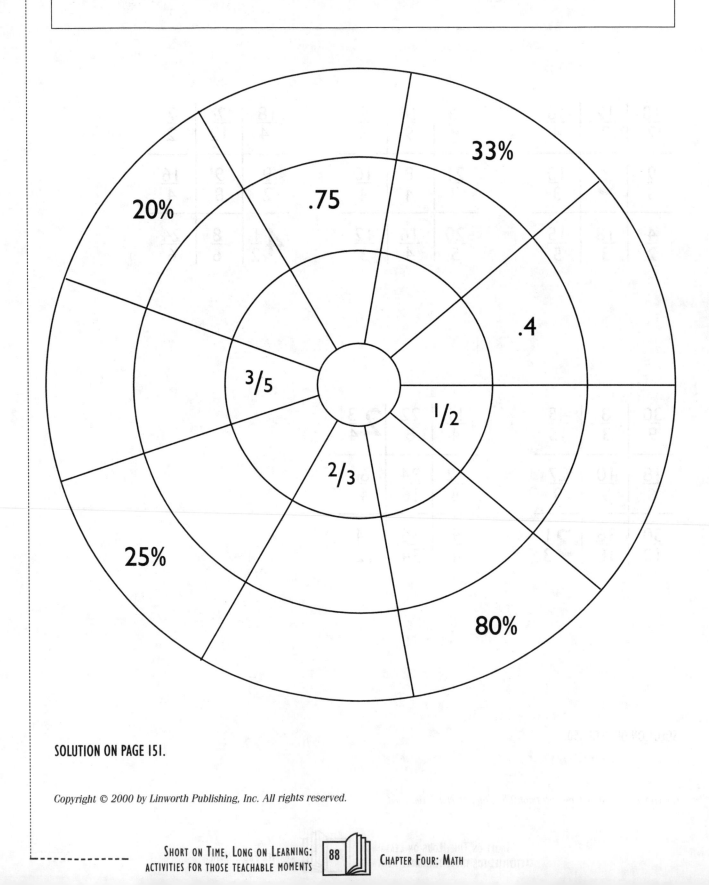

SOLUTION ON PAGE 151.

TRAVELING TIME

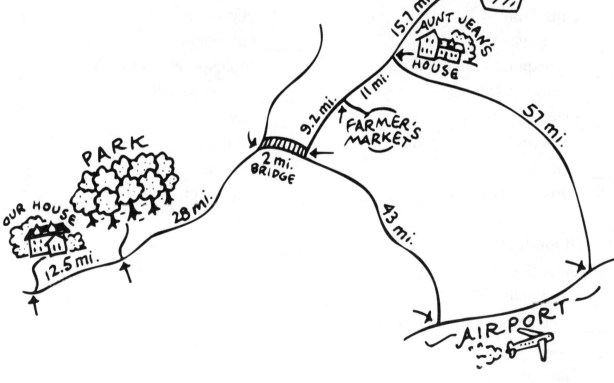

How to Play!

Study the map below, then calculate the shortest distance to the following:

The distance from our house to Aunt Jean's house _____

The distance from the Farmer's Market to the park entrance _____

The distance from Aunt Jean's house to town and then to the Farmer's Market _____

The distance from our house to the airport _____

CHALLENGE: Calculate the speed for each of these by car, bike, and walking. Determine ahead of time a likely speed (for example, 35 miles per hour by car).

SOLUTION ON PAGE 151.

A TASTY TREAT

Here are the ingredients to make 12 blueberry muffins:

2 cups flour

$1/4$ cup sugar

1 tablespoon baking powder

$1/2$ teaspoon salt

1 egg

1 cup milk

$1/4$ cup oil

1 cup blueberries

YUM!

Calculate how much of each ingredient you would need to:

Double the recipe:

_____ cups flour

_____ cup sugar

_____ tablespoons baking powder

_____ teaspoon salt

_____ eggs

_____ cups milk

_____ cup oil

_____ cups blueberries

Divide the recipe in half:

_____ cup flour

_____ cup sugar

_____ tablespoon baking powder

_____ teaspoon salt

_____ egg

_____ cup milk

_____ cup oil

_____ cup blueberries

Make 18 muffins:

_____ cups flour

_____ cup sugar

_____ tablespoons baking powder

_____ teaspoon salt

_____ eggs

_____ cups milk

_____ cup oil

_____ cups blueberries

SOLUTION ON PAGE 151

THREE KINDS OF NUMBERS

Solve the problems below.

A. $2 \times \dfrac{1}{3} =$ _____

B. $\dfrac{3}{4} \times 7 =$ _____

C. $\dfrac{1}{2} \times 4 =$ _____

D. $3 \times \dfrac{5}{6} =$ _____

E. $\dfrac{2}{7} \times 3 =$ _____

F. $\dfrac{5}{8} \times 8 =$ _____

G. $8 \times \dfrac{7}{12} =$ _____

H. $\dfrac{4}{5} \times 5 =$ _____

I. $5 \times \dfrac{2}{9} =$ _____

J. $3 \times \dfrac{3}{10} =$ _____

Now color the squares below this way:

If your answer was a whole number, color the square with its letter yellow.

If your answer was a fraction, color it red.

If your answer was a mixed number, color it blue.

When you are finished, you will have a picture of a future helper.

L	U	T	N	X	Y	A	E	J	O	M	R	Z	O	P	M	Y
W	M	Z	S	N	C	H	F	H	C	R	V	P	K	Q	O	R
V	N	T	X	J	F	E	H	J	H	A	Y	W	Z	W	U	K
U	L	P	O	E	C	F	H	C	F	J	V	L	X	Q	R	M
Z	Y	T	P	Z	H	A	J	E	C	Z	N	S	R	X	V	O
W	O	V	P	S	F	H	F	C	H	R	T	Z	L	M	U	X
Y	J	E	K	X	O	G	B	D	T	W	Z	N	Y	S	N	O
L	B	D	R	B	I	G	D	B	G	I	K	L	M	U	L	Y
V	I	G	X	I	G	D	B	D	I	G	W	Y	R	O	X	Q
N	D	B	I	D	B	C	F	H	G	D	B	G	I	D	A	V
W	G	I	B	B	G	H	C	A	B	G	I	D	B	G	E	X
X	Z	L	Y	I	G	F	H	C	D	I	V	L	P	Y	U	R
T	N	O	U	G	D	H	C	F	B	I	W	R	T	M	N	S
P	V	S	M	B	D	I	G	I	D	B	Y	T	N	X	O	P
V	N	W	N	G	I	D	B	I	G	D	U	Z	O	S	Y	W
R	L	Q	R	D	B	I	G	B	D	I	M	P	V	W	K	X
U	X	K	R	Z	B	D	O	I	G	N	T	Y	M	Q	P	V
Y	L	U	W	P	G	I	T	D	B	R	X	S	V	Z	L	W
S	Q	X	Z	H	F	C	Z	C	H	F	S	L	T	K	S	N

SOLUTION ON PAGE 152.

CHAPTER 5

Music

LISTEN CLOSELY

■ **PARTICIPATION:** Class

■ **MATERIALS:** tape player or CD player, tape or CD of classical music

How to Play!

Listen carefully. See how many instruments can be identified.

RHYTHM BEAT

■ **PARTICIPATION:** Class

How to Play!

Clap a rhythm. Class repeats. Increase the complexity.

NAME THAT TUNE

■ **PARTICIPATION:** Class

How to Play!

One student hums the first part of a song. The rest of the class must guess the song.

★ INTRODUCING . . .

■ **PARTICIPATION:** Class

■ **MATERIALS:** short biographies of famous composers. Here are some sources: *Lives of the Musicians* by Kathleen Krull (Harcourt, 1993), *Who and When* series by Sarah Halliwell (Raintree/Steck-Vaughn, 1998), *Twenty Names in Classical Music* by Alan Blackwood (Marshall Cavendish, 1988), *Twenty Names in Pop Music* by Andrew Langley (Marshall Cavendish, 1988).

How to Play!

Read the biography of one composer each day for a week or two.

CHALLENGE: At the end of the time, read a short line or two and ask students to identify the composer.

GETTING TO KNOW . . .

■ **PARTICIPATION:** Class

■ **MATERIALS:** tapes or CDs of a wide range of music and a tape or CD player. Try symphonies, solo vocal, chorus, solo piano, instrumental quartets, marching bands, musicals, spirituals, opera, jazz, country, pop, rock, and blues.

How to Play!

Play a short selection with the students listening (not as background music to another activity). Discuss similarities and differences with pieces you have heard in the past, types of instruments or voices used, rhythms, harmonies, and emotional response.

WHAT A BEAUTIFUL SOUND

■ **PARTICIPATION:** Class

■ **MATERIALS:** chart of instruments of the orchestra or individual pictures of the instruments

How to Play!

Give a short description. Students must identify the correct instrument.

CHALLENGE: Call out "string," "woodwind," "brass," or "percussion." Students must identify instruments within that category.

KNOW YOUR SYMBOLS

■ **PARTICIPATION:** Class

■ **MATERIALS:** cards with musical symbols printed on them (e.g., whole note, half note, quarter note, eighth note, sixteenth note, dotted half note, dotted quarter note, whole rest, half rest, quarter rest, eighth rest, sixteenth rest, treble clef, bass clef, measure, sharp, flat, natural, repeat sign, crescendo, decrescendo, and tie).

■ **ADVANCE PREPARATION:** If you do not have preprinted cards, draw the symbols on cards.

How to Play!

Students must identify the symbol.

CHALLENGE: Students must show the symbol in a piece of sheet music.

 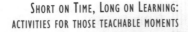

IN HARMONY

■ **PARTICIPATION:** Class

How to Play!

On a piano or keyboard, play some examples of melody, harmony, or dissonance. Have the students identify.

RANGE

■ **PARTICIPATION:** Class

■ **MATERIALS:** tapes or CDs of vocal performers from each range (soprano, alto, tenor, and baritone) and a tape or CD player

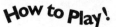
How to Play!

Play the tape or CDs, pointing out each vocal range.

 CHALLENGE: Students will identify vocal ranges on other tapes or CDs.

CAN IT BE DONE?

■ **PARTICIPATION:** Class/Individuals

■ **MATERIALS:** paper and pencil

How to Play!

Take one sentence of a song lyric and diagram it.

FINISH IT

■ **PARTICIPATION:** Class/Individuals

■ **ADVANCE PREPARATION:** On the board, write several time signatures on staffs. Draw a note or rest on each.

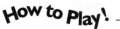
How to Play!

Have the students, as a class or individually, complete the measure.

MUSICAL FAMILIES

How to Play!

Place the musical instruments of the orchestra in the correct family.

STRINGS	WOODWIND	BRASS	PERCUSSION
_____	_____	_____	_____
_____	_____	_____	_____
_____	_____	_____	_____
_____	_____	_____	_____
_____	_____	_____	_____

bass   bassoon   bells   cello
chimes   clarinet   cornet   cymbal
drum   flute   French horn   harp
oboe   piccolo   xylophone   trombone
trumpet   tuba   viola   violin

SOLUTION ON PAGE 152.

A MUSICAL WORD

How to Play!

Using the clue below, write a word that means something else in music.

Fits in a lock _____

Do this to a car engine _____

A red vegetable _____

Peace _____

You speak with this. _____

Drama on a stage _____

You turn this up or down on the TV . _____

A girl's name _____

Black _____

SOLUTION ON PAGE 152.

WHAT'S THAT SYMBOL?

How to Play!

Match the symbol with the word that describes it.

Treble clef

Repeat

Staccato

Crescendo

Hold

Bass clef

Slur

Accent

Decrescendo

SOLUTION ON PAGE 152.

MUSICAL LADDERS

How to Play!

On each step of the ladder, write the words in order.

VOICES

_____ (highest)

_____

_____

_____ (lowest)

GROUPS

_____ (fewest)

_____

_____

_____ (most)

TEMPO

_____ (fastest)

_____

_____

_____

_____ (slowest)

VOICES	GROUPS	TEMPO
alto	duet	allegro
baritone	quartet	andante
soprano	solo	largo
tenor	trio	moderato
		presto

SOLUTION ON PAGE 153.

Copyright © 2000 by Linworth Publishing, Inc. All rights reserved.

FAMOUS COMPOSERS

How to Play!

Find the names of the composers (last name only) in the puzzle below. The names may be across, down, or diagonal. After you have circled all the names, the letters that are left will spell out a message about one of the composers.

Johann Sebastian BACH
Ludwig van BEETHOVEN
Georges BIZET
Johannes BRAHMS
Claude DEBUSSY
Antonin DVORAK
Edvard GRIEG
George Frideric HANDEL
Franz Joseph HAYDN

Franz LISZT
Gustav MAHLER
Felix MENDELSSOHN
Wolfgang Amadeus MOZART
Sergei PROKOFIEV
Giacomo PUCCINI
Maurice RAVEL
Allessandro SCARLATTI

Franz SCHUBERT
Robert SCHUMANN
Richard STRAUSS
Pyotr Ilyitch TCHAIKOVSKY
Giuseppe VERDI
Antonio VIVALDI
Richard WAGNER
Carl Maria von WEBER

```
N  M  B  O  S  C  A  R  L  A  T  T  I
I  D  L  A  V  I  V  Z  A  R  C  T  A
D  C  Y  H  C  N  N  A  M  U  H  C  S
E  G  I  A  L  H  D  P  R  A  A  B  O
B  E  E  T  H  O  V  E  N  D  I  T  P
U  I  I  G  Z  S  D  Y  Z  K  R  U
S  R  V  W  A  S  E  S  E  C  O  E  C
S  G  O  E  U  L  I  T  M  K  V  B  C
Y  P  T  A  R  E  O  L  O  S  S  U  I
K  A  R  O  V  D  I  F  E  N  K  H  N
G  T  A  M  U  N  I  S  I  V  Y  C  I
S  C  Z  A  R  E  N  G  A  W  A  S  T
A  G  O  E  V  M  F  S  M  H  A  R  B
O  U  M  A  H  L  E  R  E  B  E  W  R
```

— — — — — — —'— — — — — — —

— — — — —'— — — —

— — — — — — — — — — — — — —

— — — — — — — — — — .

SOLUTION ON PAGE 153.

PATRIOTIC SONGS

How to Play!

Match the notes and rests below to identify a famous song, the date it was written, who wrote the lyrics, and where it was written.

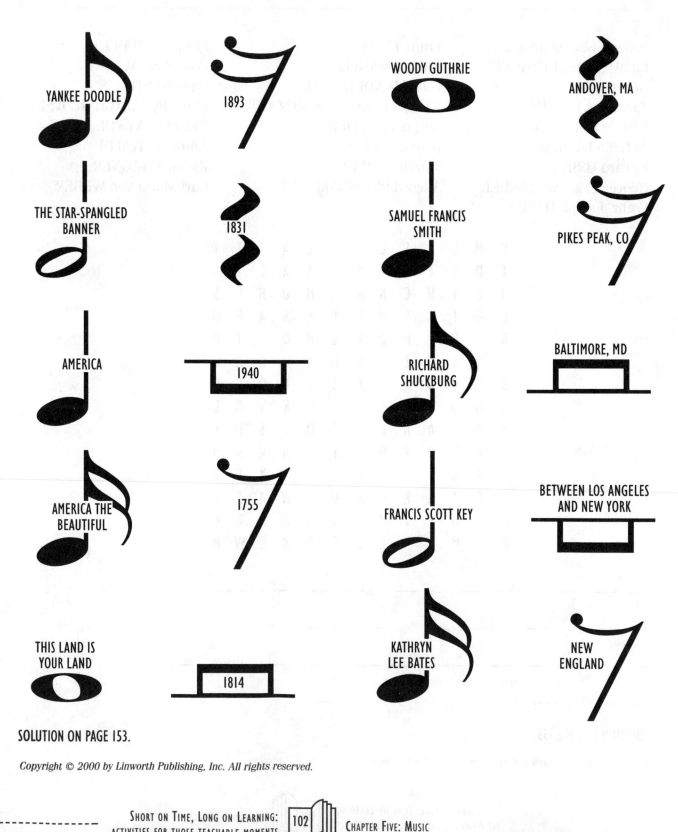

YANKEE DOODLE

1893

WOODY GUTHRIE

ANDOVER, MA

THE STAR-SPANGLED BANNER

1831

SAMUEL FRANCIS SMITH

PIKES PEAK, CO

AMERICA

1940

RICHARD SHUCKBURG

BALTIMORE, MD

AMERICA THE BEAUTIFUL

1755

FRANCIS SCOTT KEY

BETWEEN LOS ANGELES AND NEW YORK

THIS LAND IS YOUR LAND

1814

KATHRYN LEE BATES

NEW ENGLAND

SOLUTION ON PAGE 153.

CHAPTER **6**

★ A PORTABLE MUSEUM

■ **PARTICIPATION:** Class

■ **MATERIALS:** art books from the library. Decide on a theme, perhaps tying in to social studies: the art of a particular time in history (ancient Rome, Middle Ages, Renaissance) or a place (China, Japan, Europe).

How to Play!

Display the book or books. Have students comment on a particular picture or artist, asking leading questions. Encourage them to look through the books on their own.

★ INTRODUCING . . .

■ **PARTICIPATION:** Class

■ **MATERIALS:** books that present a short biography of an artist. Some sources: *Lives of the Artists* by Kathleen Krull (Harcourt, 1995), *Who and When* series by Sarah Halliwell (Raintree/Steck-Vaughn, 1998), *Twenty Names in Art* by Alan Blackwood (Marshall Cavendish, 1988).

How to Play!

Read about one artist. Discuss his life and impact on the world.

★ NOW YOU SEE IT

■ **PARTICIPATION:** Class

■ **MATERIALS:** a book featuring optical illusions. Try these sources: *You Won't Believe Your Eyes* (National Geographic Society, 1987), *101 Amazing Optical Illusions* by Terry Jennings (Sterling, 1996), *Astounding Optical Illusions* by Katherine Joyce (Sterling, 1994), or the *Magic Eye* books. Ask your librarian for additional suggestions.

How to Play!

Show the class some famous optical illusions. Encourage them to find more.

GRAPHIC DESIGN

PARTICIPATION: Class

ADVANCE PREPARATION: Collect samples of work by graphic artists or designers, for example, magazine ads, restaurant menus, signs, pictures of gardens, CD covers, book covers, and food packages.

How to Play!

Discuss line, color, and pattern in the examples.

LINES

PARTICIPATION: Class

MATERIALS: paper and pencil

ADVANCE PREPARATION: Find some examples in print media of lines of various types. Bring in some books of famous artwork that illustrate various types of lines.

How to Play!

Discuss the examples.

CHALLENGE: Have the students use various types of lines to draw forms, movement, or emotion.

SHAPES

PARTICIPATION: Class

MATERIALS: paper and pencil

ADVANCE PREPARATION: Search the print media for examples of shapes. Display some books of famous artwork that illustrate various shapes.

How to Play!

Discuss the examples.

CHALLENGE: Have the students use various types of shapes to draw faces, bodies, and buildings.

COLOR

- ■ PARTICIPATION: Class

- ■ MATERIALS: paper and crayons

- ■ ADVANCE PREPARATION: Bring in some examples of use of color in print media. Check out some library books of famous artwork that illustrate color.

How to Play!

Discuss the examples. Point out warm and cool colors, color combinations, and color mixing.

CHALLENGE: Have the students experiment with color in their own drawings.

PATTERNS

- ■ PARTICIPATION: Class

- ■ MATERIALS: paper and pencil

How to Play!

Discuss patterns in nature, construction, and the classroom. Have the students draw a line or shape on paper, then draw the same line or shape to make a pattern, then change the pattern in size, orientation, or shape.

IT'S ALL ART

- ■ PARTICIPATION: Class

How to Play!

Ask the students what they think of when they hear the word "art." On the board, make a list of objects or techniques that can be art, thinking beyond the usual painting and sculpture. (Ideas: Photography, clothing design, embroidery, beadwork, knitting, weaving of cloth or baskets, jewelry design, furniture design.)

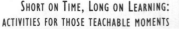

PICTURE GRAPH

- ■ **PARTICIPATION:** Class/Partners/Individuals
- ■ **MATERIALS:** graph paper, pencil
- ■ **ADVANCE PREPARATION:** Draw a fairly simple picture on the board (or have a student draw it).

How to Play!

Give each student a piece of graph paper. Then draw graph lines over the picture on the board. Have the students transfer the picture to their individual papers by drawing the same line that is in a square on the board on a square of their graph paper.

★ LOOK CLOSELY

- ■ **PARTICIPATION:** Class/Individuals
- ■ **MATERIALS:** books by Al Hirschfeld and Marc Brown

Caricaturist Al Hirschfeld hides his daughter Nina's name in his drawings. Children's author/illustrator Marc Brown hides his children's and other names in his early *Arthur* books.

How to Play!

Show examples.

 CHALLENGE: Have children draw a picture that contains their name hidden in it.

LET ME GIVE YOU MY CARD

- ■ **PARTICIPATION:** Class/Individuals
- ■ **MATERIALS:** business cards and pens, markers, or crayons

How to Play!

Use the backs of business cards to make class or individual business cards with names and symbols or logos.

DO AS I SAY

■ PARTICIPATION: Partners

■ MATERIALS: paper and pencil

How to Play!

One student describes while the other draws. He will describe a thing without telling what the thing is and telling only what to draw in terms of lines, shapes, and direction.

IT'S BACKWARD

■ PARTICIPATION: Individuals

■ MATERIALS: mirror, paper, and pencil

How to Play!

Have the students print or write a word or phrase backward. Hold it up to the mirror to read.

YOU BE THE DESIGNER

■ PARTICIPATION: Individuals

■ MATERIALS: paper, pencil, markers

How to Play!

Challenge the students to design a new stamp.

IT'S A PLAN

■ PARTICIPATION: Individuals

■ MATERIALS: graph paper, pencil

How to Play!

Instruct the students to design a room on graph paper. Remember to put in windows and doors!

 CHALLENGE: Calculate how big the room will be and write on the paper how many inches or feet each square represents.

FORM AND DESIGN

■ **PARTICIPATION:** Individuals

■ **MATERIALS:** paper and pencil

How to Play!

Using the printed letters of the alphabet, draw a building.

A MINI-MOVIE

■ **PARTICIPATION:** Individuals

■ **MATERIALS:** a very small tablet of paper for each student (Post-it® notes are great!)

How to Play!

Have students draw a simple picture on each page with each picture just slightly different than the one before so movement, change, or action can be shown to take place as the tablet is flipped through.

A COLORFUL PUZZLE

On each line of the rainbow below is a common color word. From the list, choose three words that are the same color and write them on the same line as the rainbow word.

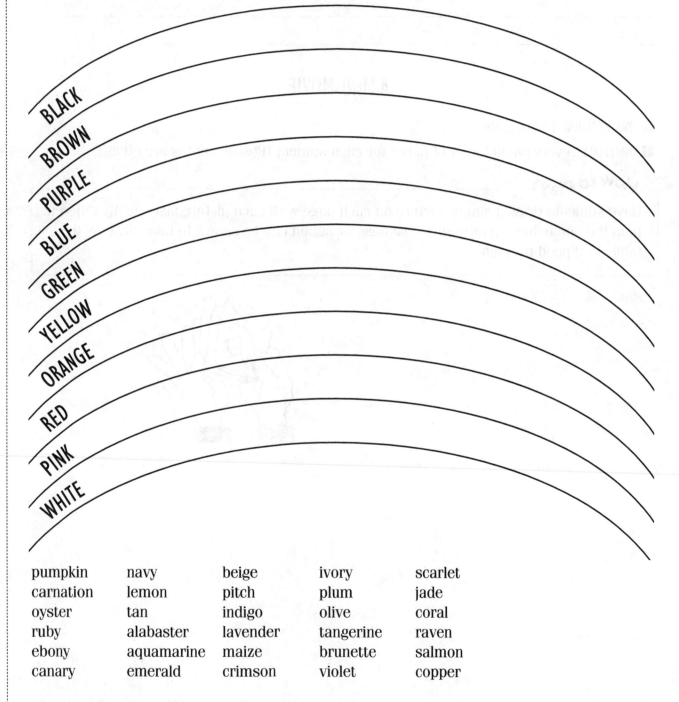

BLACK

BROWN

PURPLE

BLUE

GREEN

YELLOW

ORANGE

RED

PINK

WHITE

pumpkin	navy	beige	ivory	scarlet
carnation	lemon	pitch	plum	jade
oyster	tan	indigo	olive	coral
ruby	alabaster	lavender	tangerine	raven
ebony	aquamarine	maize	brunette	salmon
canary	emerald	crimson	violet	copper

SOLUTION ON PAGE 154.

MAKE A SHAPE

Next to each word, draw a line or shape that illustrates the word. Be creative! There is no one right answer here!

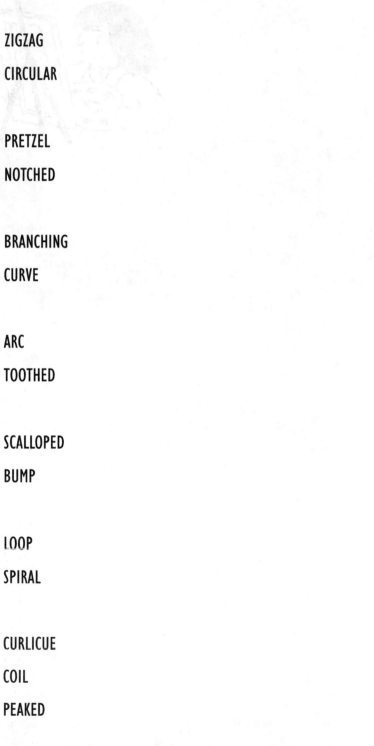

ZIGZAG

CIRCULAR

PRETZEL

NOTCHED

BRANCHING

CURVE

ARC

TOOTHED

SCALLOPED

BUMP

LOOP

SPIRAL

CURLICUE

COIL

PEAKED

WHAT CAN AN ARTIST USE?

Unscramble each word below to spell the name of something an artist may use to draw or paint.

1. naryoc

2. epn

3. napit

4. khacl

5. ilo tanip

6. preetam

7. slepat

8. neclip

9. trowalorec

10. sperto antip

11. axw

12. clarcoha

SOLUTION ON PAGE 154.

20TH CENTURY ARTISTS

How to Play!

Using the code below, write the name of the artist who did the following:

SCULPTURE—FIGURES

$\underline{\quad}$ $\underline{\quad}$ $\underline{\quad}$ $\underline{\quad}$ $\underline{\quad}$ $\quad$ $\underline{\quad}$ $\underline{\quad}$ $\underline{\quad}$ $\underline{\quad}$ $\underline{\quad}$
    "   &   # $]   '   \   \ $ &

SCULPTURE—MOBILES

    *   )   &   ]   *   #   —   & $ ^   *   )   —   & $

PHOTOGRAPHY

    &   —   !   * $ —   /   ~   &   =   ^   "   &   #

PHOTOGRAPHY—SOCIAL DOCUMENTARY

    —   \ $ \   ~   "   &   *   )   *   #   (&

ILLUSTRATION—MAGAZINE COVERS

    #   \ $ '   *   # $ \   ^   :   !   &   )   )

PAINTING—SEMI-ABSTRACT

    (&   \ $ (=   *   \   :   &   &   @   @   &

PAINTING—CUBISM

    +   *   [   )   \   +   =   ^   *   /   /   \

ACTION PAINTING

    %   *   ^   :   /   \   #   +   \   )   )   \   ^   :

PAINTING—REALISM

    *   #   — $ &   !   !   ]   &   ~   "

PAINTING—POP

    $ \   ]   )   =   ^   "   ~   &   #   /   ~   &   =   #

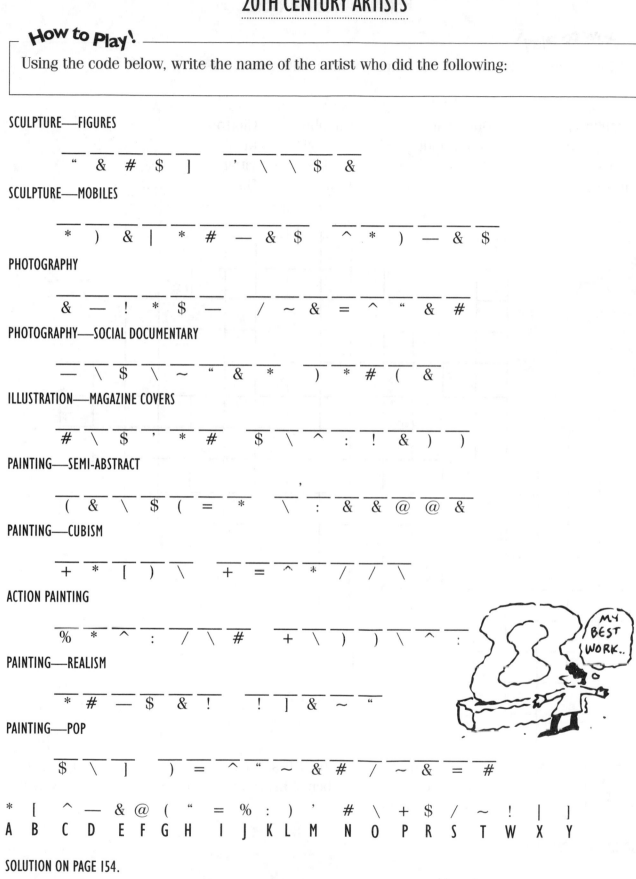

*	[	^	—	&	@	(	"	=	%	:	)	'	#	\	+	$	/	~	!				
A	B	C	D	E	F	G	H	I	J	K	L	M	N	O	P	R	S	T	W	X	Y

SOLUTION ON PAGE 154.

RENAISSANCE PAINTERS

How to Play!

Fill in the puzzle below with the names of the painters in the list.

Brunelleschi   Donatello   Cimabue   Giotto
Michelangelo   Rembrandt   DaVinci   Rubens
Botticelli   Bruegel   El Greco   Titian
Tintoretto   Cellini   Holbein   Durer

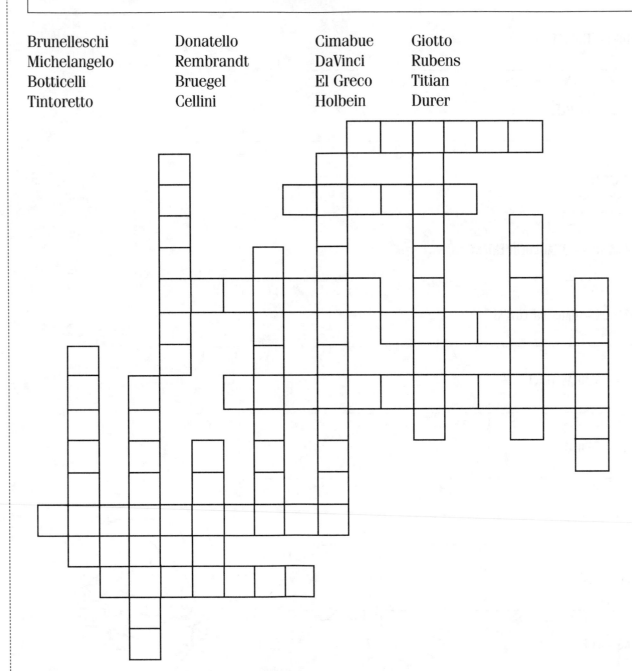

 CHALLENGE: Some artists are known by their first name (Rembrandt, Michelangelo) and some by their last name (DaVinci, Rubens). Learn more about the artists above. What would be a good source to use?

SOLUTION ON PAGE 155.

 # Thinking Skills/ Problem Solving

TOOL TIME

■ PARTICIPATION: Class

■ MATERIALS: a simple tool, such as a compass, tape measure, carpenter's square, level, vise, clamp, plane, palette knife, glue gun, pliers, brush, binoculars, press, needle threader, apple corer, scale, timer, peeler, mortar and pestle, coffee mill, pepper mill, egg beater, sieve, scale, or any tool used in a workshop, kitchen, or home

■ ADVANCE PREPARATION: Bring tool in plus any materials needed with it, such as an apple for the apple corer.

How to Play!

Ask how the tool might be used. Demonstrate its use. Ask if there are any similar tools. Might it have been used in the past? If not, what was used in its place?

MEMORY BOOSTERS

■ PARTICIPATION: Class

How to Play!

Talk about common memory aids, for example, H O M E S for the names of the Great Lakes or N E W S for the directions north, east, west, south. Have the students make up their own for other lists of words that they need to memorize now.

WHAT ELSE CAN I BE?

■ PARTICIPATION: Class

■ MATERIALS: large sheet of paper and marker

■ ADVANCE PREPARATION: Write these subjects on a sheet of paper or the board: History, geography, civics, reading, writing, speech, math, science, art, music

How to Play!

Discuss what careers people might choose if they are interested in a certain subject.

 CHALLENGE: Discuss crossover; for example, a landscape designer may have interests in art and math.

SOLUTION ON PAGE 155.

★ ALL IN PLACE

■ PARTICIPATION: Class

■ MATERIALS: large sheet of paper and marker

How to Play!

As a class, make a list entitled "How We Organize." Include any organizational pattern in society: Books in the library, names in a phone book, foods in a grocery store, and so on.

★ A NEW USE

■ PARTICIPATION: Class

How to Play!

Tell the students: Sometimes buildings are abandoned, but still usable. Think of new uses for an abandoned school, church, stadium, shopping mall, office building, apartment building, restaurant, or post office. Discuss. Concentrate on the special features each building includes.

★ BE CREATIVE

■ PARTICIPATION: Class

■ MATERIALS: the following objects or a list of them

Paper clips	Paper bags
Pencils	Plastic bags
String	Egg cartons
Wastebaskets	Microwave dinner dishes
Foil	Paper tubes
Buttons	Old greeting cards
Marbles	(any other familiar object)

How to Play!

Think of as many new uses as possible for these items.

IT'S FUN!

■ **PARTICIPATION:** Class

■ **MATERIALS:** paper, pencil, large sheet of paper, and marker

How to Play!

As a class, come up with a list of 10-20 activities, such as reading, playing sports, or watching TV. Have each person in the class write down the activities in ranked order with the activity they enjoy most at the top. Then make a chart or graph of "Favorite Activities of Our Class."

★ LOOK INTO THE FUTURE

■ **PARTICIPATION:** Class

How to Play!

ASK: What class will you be? (High School Class of [year])

How old will you be in [name a year]?

ALIKE? DIFFERENT?

■ **PARTICIPATION:** Class

■ **MATERIALS:** paper and pencil

How to Play!

Write one of the following categories on the board: *Nature, man-made, grows, can be counted, is usually green, only in big cities, or seen in one season.* Instruct students to write down the name of one object that this category brings to mind. Next, divide students into groups of five. Have them compare what they have written. What are the similarities (besides the category)? What are the differences?

SURPRISE!

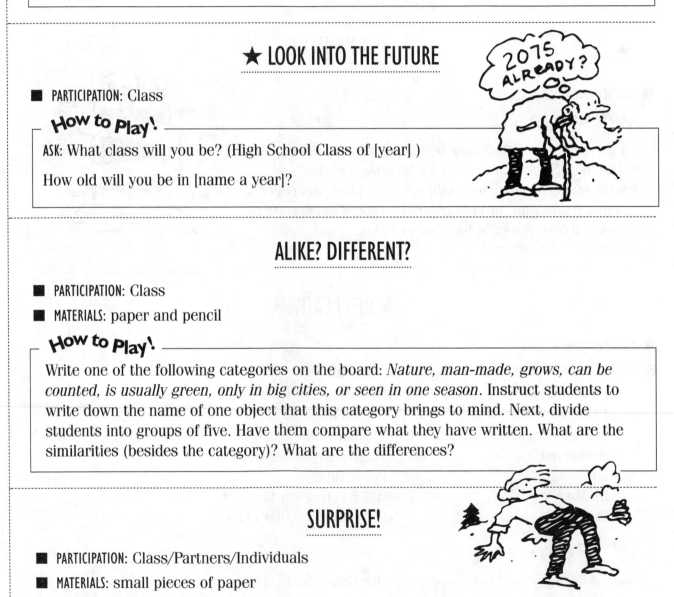

■ **PARTICIPATION:** Class/Partners/Individuals

■ **MATERIALS:** small pieces of paper

■ **ADVANCE PREPARATION:** Write on a piece of paper a motion or activity that can be acted out (Examples: Walk like a crab, do five jumping jacks, pick an apple).

How to Play!

Have partners or individual students pick a piece of paper and act out what it says.

FINISH IT

- **PARTICIPATION:** Class/Partners/Individuals
- **ADVANCE PREPARATION:** Write on the board y, y, h, l, y, . . .
    Write on the board S, M, T, W, . . .
    Write on the board 3, 3, 5, 4, . . .

How to Play!

Ask the students to finish the sequence and explain it.

SOLUTION ON PAGE 156.

ALL FOR ONE

- **PARTICIPATION:** Class/Partners/Individuals
- **ADVANCE PREPARATION:** Write these words on the board:

tornado	hurricane	blizzard
maritime	tide	ocean
covey	gaggle	flock
enamel	molar	dentine
trolley	el	tram
docking	touchdown	liftoff
bow	loop	half-hitch
tower	spire	steeple
juror	counselor	judge
curtain	scene	rehearsal

How to Play!

Ask the students why each set of three words belongs together.

WHAT WILL IT BE?

- **PARTICIPATION:** Class/Partners/Individuals
- **MATERIALS:** paper and pencil, if needed

How to Play!

Make a list: "The Top 10 . . ." (Movies Our Class Likes, Snack Foods, Books We Read This Year, or others as suggested).

ABRACADABRA

■ PARTICIPATION: Class/Partners/Individuals

How to Play!

Ask: Can you change six to 10? Write "six" on the board, then three lines under it:

six

————

————

————

(Here's the solution: Change one letter in each word: six, sin, tin, ten)

CHALLENGE: Have the students make up their own "changes."

★ BE CONCISE!

■ PARTICIPATION: Class/Individuals

■ MATERIALS: paper and pencil (optional)

How to Play!

Select one student to describe an object in 15 words or less. Other students must guess what it is.

★ BUT WILL IT DO WINDOWS?

■ PARTICIPATION: Class/Individuals

■ MATERIALS: paper and pencil (optional)

How to Play!

Robots are used in factories to perform monotonous or dangerous jobs. Ask: What kind of robot would be practical for household tasks? What special features would it need for different living situations? Discuss as a class or have students write.

★ WHAT WOULD YOU DO?

■ PARTICIPATION: Class/Individuals

How to Play!

ASK THE STUDENTS: If a day consisted of 48 hours instead of 24, what would you do? What if it consisted of 12 hours?

★ STRANDED

■ PARTICIPATION: Class/Individuals

How to Play!

DISCUSS: You are on a desert island. What would you want with you? Remember, there is no electricity!

★ HERE WE GO!

■ PARTICIPATION: Class/Individuals

How to Play!

DISCUSS: You are packing a suitcase for a trip. What do you take if you are going to: An overnight visit to your grandparents? A trip to climb Mount Everest? A charitable trip to a Third World country? A one week flight on the space shuttle? A trip to Sweden in the winter? A trip to Texas in the summer?

★ THINK FAST

■ PARTICIPATION: Class/Individuals

How to Play!

Ask the students:
Can you think of five body parts that start with the letter E?
What are five animals that begin with the letter T?
Name five ways of getting around that are four letters or less.
Can you think of five pieces of clothing that start with the letter S?
What are five computer terms that can also mean something else?
Can you think of five foods that are three letters long?
Name five sports that are played indoors.

SOLUTION ON PAGE 156.

FOR EASE OR COMFORT

■ PARTICIPATION: Partners/Individuals

■ MATERIALS: paper and pencil

How to Play!

Have the students design a piece of furniture or tool that is usable, then describe it to the class.

SELL IT

PARTICIPATION: Partners/Individuals

MATERIALS: paper and pencils or markers

How to Play!

Make up ads for something used in school or for subjects studied in school.

AN OLD FAVORITE

■ PARTICIPATION: Partners/Individuals

■ MATERIALS: paper and pencil

How to Play!

Have the students make new rules for a favorite board game (e.g., Monopoly, Scrabble, Risk).

★ YUMMY

■ PARTICIPATION: Individuals

■ MATERIALS: paper and pencil

How to Play!

Have students think up a new flavor of ice cream, a new cereal, a new type of doughnut, a new topping for pizza, or a new kind of cookie.

★ WHY?

PARTICIPATION: Individuals

MATERIALS: paper and pencil

How to Play!

Have students complete the sentence: "I wonder why. . . ." Discuss in class, allowing other students to answer. If no one knows, discuss how you might go about finding an answer.

A PICTURE IS WORTH . . .

PARTICIPATION: Individuals

MATERIALS: newspapers and magazines

ADVANCE PREPARATION: Cut out pictures or photographs.

How to Play!

Have students select one picture that appeals to them. Have them write a one- or two-sentence caption for the photo. Be creative.

LINE DESIGN

PARTICIPATION: Individuals

MATERIALS: paper and pencil

How to Play!

Have the students print as many words as they can, using only capital letters with curves and then print as many words as they can, using only capital letters with straight lines.

GREEK AND ROMAN GODDESSES

How to Play!

Fill in the puzzle with the names of the goddesses below. Each puzzle will have one Greek goddess, one Roman goddess, and a word that tells what they protected or what they were.

GREEK	ROMAN	FAMOUS FOR
Artemis	Diana	hunt
Hestia	Vesta	hearth
Aphrodite	Venus	love
Eos	Aurora	dawn
Athena	Minerva	wisdom
Hera	Juno	queen
Fates	Parcae	life
Demeter	Ceres	agriculture

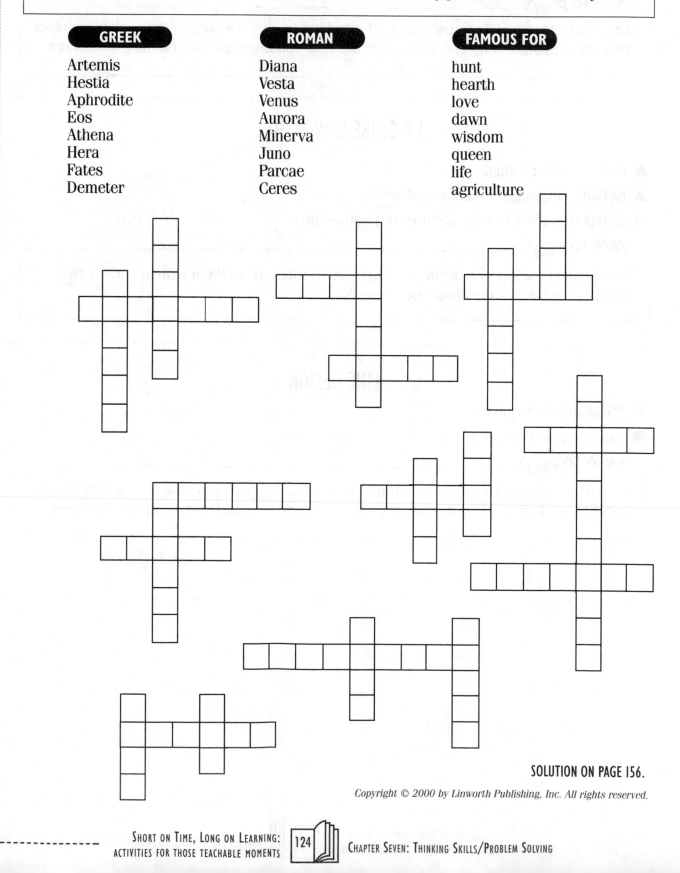

SOLUTION ON PAGE 156.

GREEK AND ROMAN GODS

How to Play!

Fill in the puzzle with the names of the gods below. Each puzzle will have one Greek god, one Roman god, and a word that tells what they protected or what they were.

GREEK	ROMAN	GOD OF
Ares	Mars	war
Hephaestus	Vulcan	fire
Cronus	Saturn	agriculture
Apollo	Apollo	poetry
Zeus	Jupiter	chief
Dionysus	Bacchus	wine
Hermes	Mercury	messenger
Poseidon	Neptune	sea
Hades	Pluto	underworld

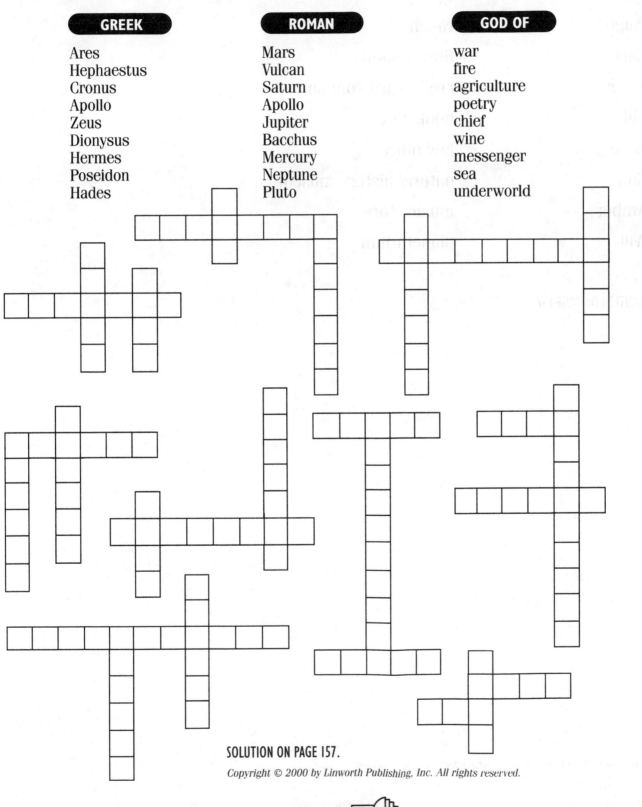

SOLUTION ON PAGE 157.

WHO WORKS WHERE?

How to Play!

Match the name of the person with the place where he works (Hint: It has to do with their names).

Paige	ranch
Carol	flower shop
Starr	credit card company
Bill	bookstore
Rose	law office
Colt	natural history museum
Amber	music store
Will	planetarium

SOLUTION ON PAGE 157.

HEAR IT!

How to Play!

Of what does each word below remind you? Name something that could make each sound. Use your imagination!

sizzle _____

crunch _____

pop _____

buzz _____

click _____

fizz _____

squish _____

splat _____

beep _____

clang _____

ding _____

hiss _____

swoosh _____

tick _____

AN INTERESTING PLACE

What would you see at:

1. an aviary? _____

2. a kennel? _____

3. a coop? _____

4. a planetarium? _____

5. an aquarium? _____

6. a culinary institute? _____

7. an equestrian show? _____

8. a masquerade? _____

9. a greenhouse? _____

10. a museum? _____

SOLUTION ON PAGE 157.

CATEGORIES A TO Z

How to Play!

As a class, pick a category. Try to think of words beginning with each letter of the alphabet that will fit.

A _____

B _____

C _____

D _____

E _____

F _____

G _____

H _____

I _____

J _____

K _____

L _____

M _____

N _____

O _____

P _____

Q _____

R _____

S _____

T _____

U _____

V _____

W _____

X _____

Y _____

Z _____

 CHALLENGE: Think of words ending with each letter of the alphabet that will fit the category.

A SPECIAL WORD

Think of the things that a mother does for her child. Write a word or phrase that begins with each letter next to the first "Mother" below. Then write a word or phrase telling what <u>a child</u> could do for his mother next to the second "Mother" below.

M _____

O _____

T _____

H _____

E _____

R _____

M _____

O _____

T _____

H _____

E _____

R _____

SOLUTION ON PAGE 158.

THINK BIG, THINK SMALL

How to Play!

For each word below, write a narrower term and a broader subject that would include it.

	NARROWER	**BROADER**
airplanes	_____	_____
beans	_____	_____
bird	_____	_____
house	_____	_____
cake	_____	_____
shirt	_____	_____
coin	_____	_____
swimming	_____	_____
rain	_____	_____
light bulb	_____	_____

SOLUTION ON PAGE 158.

ABBREVIATION WORD SEARCH

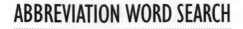

How to Play!

Find the abbreviation and the word it stands for in the puzzle below. They may be across, down, diagonal, backward or forward. Circle the words. The two words that go together will be connected to each other in some way. But there is one set that will not—because they have no letters in common!

MR	DR	RAILROAD	OCTOBER
ST	OCT	SQUARE	DOZEN
CO	IN	DOCTOR	PACKAGE
KM	LB	STREET	NUMBER
PKG	DOZ	SOUTHWEST	MONDAY
MON	DEPT	INCH	MISTER
FT	NO	POUND	TABLESPOON
OZ	RR	KILOMETER	COMPANY
SQ	TBSP	DEPARTMENT	TOUCHDOWN
TD	SW	OUNCE	FOOT

```
P  A  C  K  A  G  E  B  E  H  Y  L
O  I  F  A  M  K  Q  D  S  N  R  M
U  T  D  O  A  P  Y  R  A  U  E  R
N  X  E  B  O  F  O  P  V  C  T  E
D  E  P  A  R  T  M  E  N  T  E  T
A  L  T  O  C  O  R  U  A  N  M  S
O  F  N  O  C  A  O  B  P  T  O  I
R  R  D  U  U  T  L  Z  S  B  L  M
L  Q  R  Q  M  E  O  C  T  S  I  O
I  I  S  P  S  B  T  B  R  M  K  N
A  N  P  D  O  E  N  E  Z  O  D
R  U  O  C  K  Z  S  R  E  R  O  A
S  O  U  T  H  W  E  S  T  Z  C  Y
N  W  O  D  H  C  U  O  T  J  N  G
```

SOLUTION ON PAGE 159.

Appendix A: Activities Especially Useful for Librarians Chart

TITLE OF ACTIVITY	PAGE NUMBER
I'm Thinking of . . .	2
One-Act	3
Time Travel	4
Can You?	5
Mix It Up	5
Happily Ever After?	6
Box Office Smash!	10
Introducing . . .	10
All the Parts	11
A World of Fun and Information	14
Get Your Answers Here	15
True or Not?	16
Hans Christian Andersen	18
Who Will It Be?	24
That Will Work	24
Famous Words	25
What Did They Wear?	26
Go West, Young Person	27
Answer the Question	28
What's in the Name?	29
Time Machine	29
You're the Reporter	30
How Will It Be?	31
Thanksgiving Match-Up	41
Too Much, Too Little	46
In the Night Sky	47
Introducing . . .	50
One Makes a Difference	51
Round Off	69
Really, Really Big	72
Introducing . . .	94
A Portable Museum	104
Introducing . . .	104
Now You See It	104
Look Closely	107
All in Place	117
A New Use	117
Be Creative	117
Look into the Future	118
Be Concise!	120
But Will It Do Windows?	120
What Would You Do?	121
Stranded	121
Here We Go!	121
Think Fast	121
Yummy	122
Why?	123

Appendix B: Solutions

CHAPTER ONE: LANGUAGE ARTS

Solution—COMMUNICATION IS THE KEY

Here are some possibilities:
Spoken language, sign language, Morse code, signal flags, drums, smoke signals, e-mail, written word (letters, books, papers, magazines), Internet, bumper stickers, hand signals, car horn, telephone, telegram, music, art, body language

Solution—TOUGH RHYMES

stuff, buff, cuff, puff, fluff, gruff
sign
foe, go, row, Joe, low, mow, no, sew, tow, woe, flow, crow, stow, grow, glow, show
knight, night, tight, sight, fight, might, light, flight, fright
beat, wheat, seat, eat, heat, meat, neat, treat, cheat
ought, bought, sought, fought, thought
stew, crew, boo, flew, moo, knew, new, rue, woo, glue, grew, chew, true, shoe
tore, bore, core, yore, lore, pore, store, wore, door, nor, floor, war, shore, chore, Thor
bait, wait, trait, Kate, sate, date, gate, fate, hate, rate, pate, mate, crate, great, state, grate
ghoul, you'll, tool, fool, cool, pool, jewel, cruel, gruel

Solution—PARTS OF SPEECH SCRAMBLE

under, from, by	soopernitip	preposition
hike, became, has listened	berv	verb
and, but, or	nuccijotnon	conjunction
dog, Washington, baseball	unno	noun
loudly, quietly, perfectly	braved	adverb
she, you, their	noropun	pronoun
hooray! oh! ugh!	jertcinintoe	interjection
a, an, the	crealit	article
tiny, colorful, best	tiedvejac	adjective

Solution—LETTER BY LETTER

1. bet met end pet net ten bed den nut mend debt bend tend dune tune mute mutt
2. paw rap par ran rat tar hat tap raw war art chap chat Iran than part cart wrath
3. joy soy toy just must jump dump sump dust stump
4. bat hog hot bog tug nut gun gnu gut wit hit lit rig hat bath boat wren bait bail hail hilt with crew high light right
5. dot nut ram ran tan can man hut ear toe doe arc oar are rat cat doer shut taut dome name moat near ream tame came into mane cane auto hunt chum scam meat neat shun cram chat chain chant scare scram stain crane match reach shunt
6. net bet arm fan ran man van vie gum mug rug ten men bum rue bug big far vet farm vane mane vine bent vent been teen vein rave quiet queen

Solution—A WORLD OF FUN AND INFORMATION

At the library, you can find <u>books</u>, <u>magazines</u>, <u>newspapers</u>, <u>videos</u>, <u>tapes</u>, and <u>microfilm</u>.

The books are divided into <u>fiction</u> (which tells a made-up story) and <u>nonfiction</u> (which is true).

To find these books, use the <u>catalog</u>.

With it, you can look up books by <u>author</u> (the person who wrote the book), <u>title</u> (the name of the book), or <u>subject</u> (what the book is about).

The books are on the <u>shelves</u>.

Nonfiction books have <u>call numbers</u>, which use the <u>Dewey decimal</u> system.

If you need help, the <u>librarian</u> will help you.

You need a <u>library card</u> to borrow books.

Bring them back on time, or you may have to pay a <u>fine</u>.

Sometimes libraries have special <u>programs</u> for kids.

Solution—GET YOUR ANSWERS HERE

Who was the tallest person ever?	*Guinness Book of World Records*
Where is a list of the presidents in order?	almanac
How do you pronounce "zoology"?	dictionary
What states border on Canada?	atlas
Where can I get my hair cut?	phone book
Where can I find out about planets?	encyclopedia

Solution—TRUE OR NOT?

F	*The Adventures of Tom Sawyer*
NF	A book about the author's experiences rafting down a river
NF	A sports statistics book
F	A story about a hockey team that exists in the author's imagination
NF	A book about Alaska, its geography, history, and people
F	An adventure story set in the Arctic Circle
F	A novel about an astronaut
NF	A guide to star-gazing
NF	A travel guide to Disney World
F	A story with Mickey Mouse as the main character
NF	A biography of Queen Elizabeth I
F	A time travel story in which a girl goes back to the 1500s
F	A book about a dog that talks
NF	An animal encyclopedia
NF	A how-to-draw book
F	A book in which the main character draws scenes that come to life

Solution—LOOK! NO VOWELS!

myrrh	It makes a trio with gold and frankincense
why	A good question to ask to find out things
fly	Gnats do this; so do 747's
gypsy	She may tell your good fortune
myth	A Greek god's or goddess' story
gym	A place to lift weights and do exercises
fry	A way to cook
pygmy	One of a short tribe
dry	A desert, a non-rainy day, a type of humor
rhythm	The "beat" of music

Solution—HANS CHRISTIAN ANDERSEN

The Little Mermaid

The Ugly Duckling

The Princess and the Pea

The Little Match Girl

The Emperor's New Clothes

The Snow Queen

The Steadfast Tin Soldier

Thumbelina

The Red Shoes

The Fir Tree

Solution—ON YOUR MARK

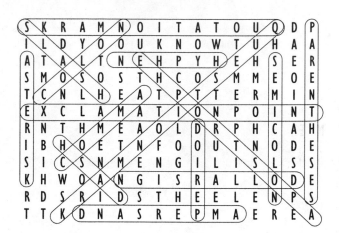

DID YOU KNOW THAT THE MOST COMMON LETTER IN THE ALPHABET FOUND IN ENGLISH WORDS IS THE LETTER E?

CHAPTER TWO: SOCIAL STUDIES

Solution—IT'S YOUR DUTY

Pay taxes, jury duty, vote, license your dog, register your car, get a driver's license, keep yard neat, obey laws

Solution—THE FOUR LARGEST

Pacific
Atlantic
Indian
Arctic

What are they? Oceans

Solution—TAKE A TRIP THROUGH CENTRAL AMERICA

Solution—EXPLORE SOUTH AMERICA

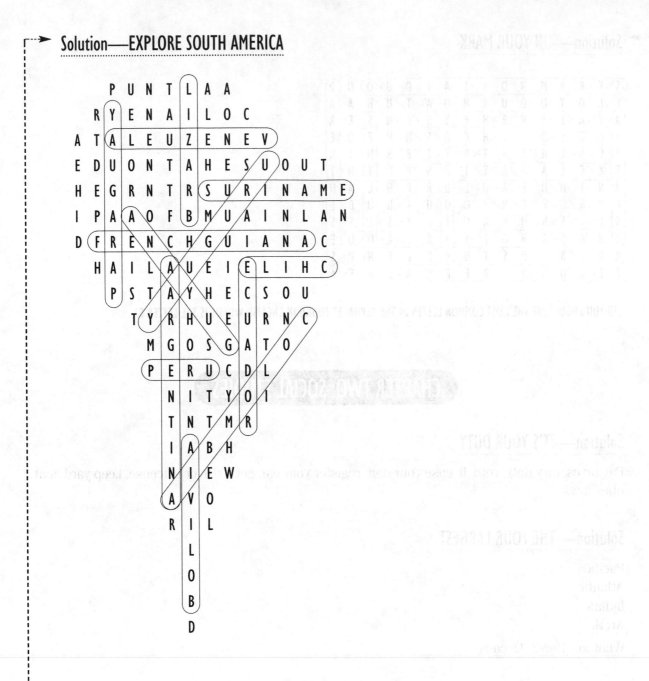

PUNTA ARENA, LOCATED ON THE SOUTHERN TIP OF MAINLAND CHILE, IS THE SOUTHERN-MOST CITY IN THE WORLD.

Solution—CATEGORIES

CONTINENTS:

A	Asia, Africa, Australia, Antarctica
E	Europe
S	South America
N	North America

COUNTRIES:

A	Afghanistan, Albania, Algeria, Andorra, Angola, Argentina, Armenia, Australia, Austria, Azerbaijan
E	Ecuador, Egypt, El Salvador, Eritrea, Estonia, Ethiopia
S	San Marino, Saudi Arabia, Senegal, Seychelles, Sierra Leone, Singapore, Slovakia, Slovenia, Somalia, South Africa, Spain, Sri Lanka, Sudan, Suriname, Swaziland, Sweden, Switzerland, Syria
N	Namibia, Nepal, Netherlands, New Zealand, Nicaragua, Niger, Nigeria, Norway

CITIES:

A	Ankara, Athens, Alexandria, Albuquerque, Atlanta, Austin
E	Essen, El Paso
S	Seoul, Sao Paulo, Shanghai, Santiago, San Francisco, Sydney, Sacramento, St. Louis, San Antonio, San Diego, San Jose, Seattle
N	New York, Naples, Nashville, New Orleans

Solution—KWANZAA

Message: AFRICAN CULTURE AND PRIDE

Solution—CANADA AND ITS CAPITALS

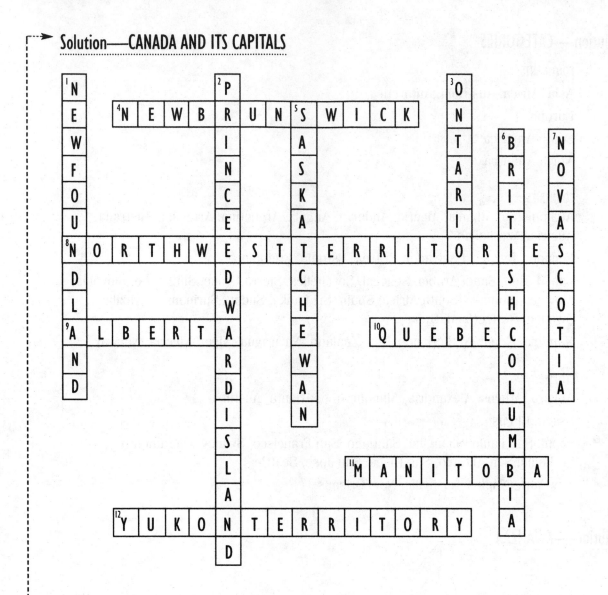

Solution—LEIF ERIKSON THE EXPLORER

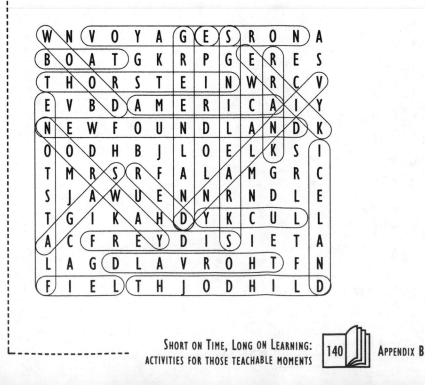

Solution—THE AGE OF EXPLORATION

		Madagascar and sea route to India	St. Lawrence River		
Bartolomeu Diaz	2E then 3S	Guiana		4S then 2W	Robert de La Salle
Vasco Nunez de Balboa	4S then 2E	around the globe	Philippines	2W 5S 1E	Hernando de Soto
Walter Raleigh	2E 2N 1W	North America		2W then 3N	Vasco da Gama
Francis Drake	2S 1E 4N		Cape of Good Hope	3S 1W 2N	Pedro Cabral
Samuel de Champlain	2E 2S 1W	Mississippi River to Louisiana	Brazil	2N 2W	John Cabot
Jacques Cartier	2E 6N		Pacific Ocean	1W 4N	Ferdinand Magellan
		Great Lakes	reaches Mississippi River		

Solution—THANKSGIVING MATCH-UP

Pilgrims set sail from England	September 1620
Pilgrims land in Massachusetts	December 1620
Pilgrims and Native Americans first celebrate Thanksgiving	Fall, 1621
Oldest American holiday	Thanksgiving
Pilgrim's ship	*Mayflower*
First president to declare a day of thanks	George Washington
English celebration at end of growing season	Harvest Home
Lydia Maria Child wrote this poem	"Over the River and through the Wood"
Cornucopia	Horn of plenty
Sarah Josepha Hale wrote to this president asking for a national Thanksgiving Day	Abraham Lincoln
Canadian Thanksgiving	Second Monday in October
United States Thanksgiving	Fourth Thursday in November

Solution—OCCUPATIONS

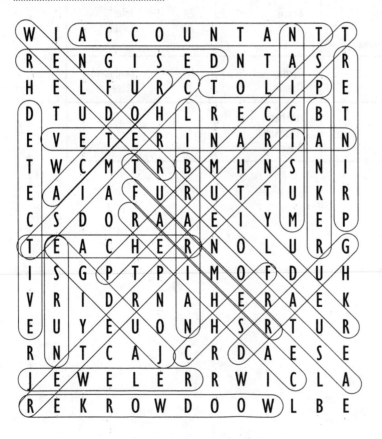

IN THE FUTURE, WHAT DO YOU THINK YOUR CAREER WILL BE?

Solution—ELECTIONS

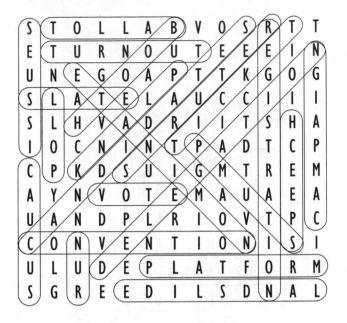

Message: VOTING — A CIVIC DUTY AND PRIVILEGE

CHAPTER THREE: SCIENCE

Solution—WEATHER WORDS

calm
clear
freezing
raining
balmy
fair
frosty

The word is: Climate.

Solution—A STORMY PUZZLE

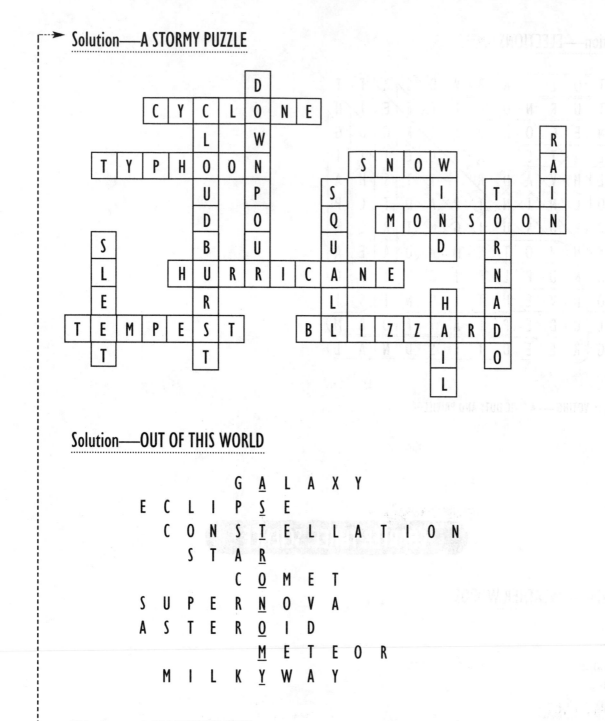

Solution—OUT OF THIS WORLD

```
              G A L A X Y
      E C L I P S E
          C O N S T E L L A T I O N
          S T A R
              C O M E T
      S U P E R N O V A
      A S T E R O I D
              M E T E O R
      M I L K Y W A Y
```

Solution—A PLANETARY QUIZ

Mercury	extreme <u>temperatures</u> from 800 degrees F to -290 degrees F
Venus	is surrounded by clouds of <u>sulfuric</u> acid
Earth	<u>water</u> covers almost three-quarters of our planet
Mars	surface is a rocky <u>desert</u>
Jupiter	its Great Red Spot is a <u>storm</u> cloud
Saturn	has <u>rings</u> made of dust and ice
Uranus	15 <u>moons</u> orbit this planet
Neptune	its moon Triton is the only one with a backward <u>orbit</u> (east to west)
Pluto	<u>smallest</u> planet of the solar system

Solution—A TO Z MAMMALS

K O A L A
A A R D V A R K
F O X
O R A N G U T A N
C A M E L
W O M B A T
G A Z E L L E
J A C K R A B B I T
L Y N X
D O L P H I N
S Q U I R R E L

Solution—WHAT'S THE DIFFERENCE?

BIRD

Warm-blooded
Two legs
Feathers
Care for young
Lives on all continents

REPTILE

Cold-blooded
Most have four legs
Scaly skin or bony shell
Some leave their eggs
Lives on all continents except Antarctica

BOTH

Has backbone
Lays eggs
Some use camouflage
Most build a nest
Lungs

Solution—WHAT'S THE DIFFERENCE II?

FISH

Has fins and tail
Breathes through gills
Most have teeth
Must live in water
Lives in every ocean, sea, lake, river

AMPHIBIAN

Most have four legs
Breathes through lungs and skin (adult)
Many have sticky tongues
Can live in water and on land
Lives on every continent except Antarctica

BOTH

Cold-blooded
Lays eggs in water
Has backbone

Solution—WHERE DO THEY BELONG?

VERTEBRATES

BIRDS	AMPHIBIANS	REPTILES	MAMMALS	FISH
dove	frog	snake	mole	shark
turkey	salamander	turtle	bat	eel
toucan	toad	gecko	whale	trout
penguin	newt	crocodile	rhinoceros	seahorse

INVERTEBRATES

INSECTS	INVERTEBRATES, NOT INSECTS
ant	sponge
bumblebee	flatworm
cockroach	clam
moth	squid

Solution—GEOLOGY ROCKS!

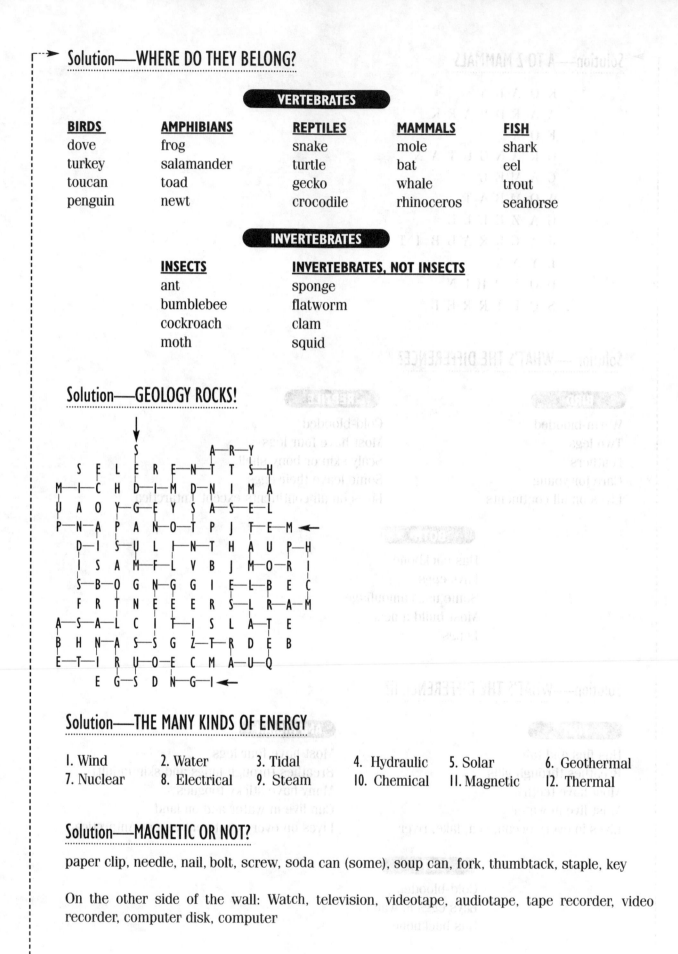

Solution—THE MANY KINDS OF ENERGY

1. Wind	2. Water	3. Tidal	4. Hydraulic	5. Solar	6. Geothermal
7. Nuclear	8. Electrical	9. Steam	10. Chemical	11. Magnetic	12. Thermal

Solution—MAGNETIC OR NOT?

paper clip, needle, nail, bolt, screw, soda can (some), soup can, fork, thumbtack, staple, key

On the other side of the wall: Watch, television, videotape, audiotape, tape recorder, video recorder, computer disk, computer

Solution—THOSE TRAVELING SEEDS

fur	animals
water	weather
plants themselves	
wind	people
clothes	feathers

```
    S T I G M A
        S E P A L
        R O O T
    S T E M
        P I S T I L
S T A M E N
        L E A F
        P E T A L
    P O L L E N
```

Solution—IT'S ALL MATTER

SOLID	**LIQUID**	**GAS**
ice	oil	oxygen
minerals	ketchup	helium
crystals	milk	nitrogen
sand	mercury	air
glass	syrup	carbon dioxide
sponge	juice	steam
sugar	shampoo	carbon monoxide
dust	blood	

Solution—INSIDE THE CELL

1. membrane
2. cytoplasm
3. mitochondria
4 ribosome
5. centrioles
6. nucleus
7. organelles

UNDER A MICROSCOPE

Solution—What Time?

5:57
2:00
11:15
6:05 p.m.

Solution—NAME THAT SHAPE

```
P E N T A G O N
C I R C L E
O C T A G O N
    R H O M B U S
        R E C T A N G L E
            T R I A N G L E
S Q U A R E
    P O L Y G O N
```

Solution—SPORT SHAPES

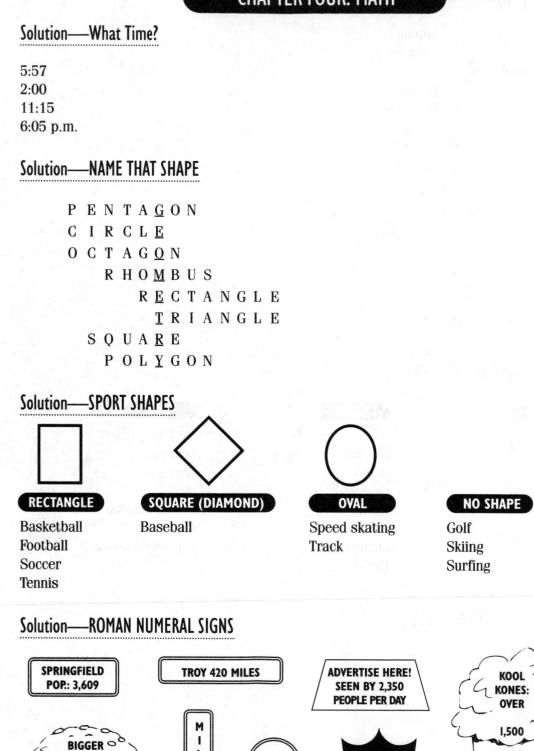

RECTANGLE
Basketball
Football
Soccer
Tennis

SQUARE (DIAMOND)
Baseball

OVAL
Speed skating
Track

NO SHAPE
Golf
Skiing
Surfing

Solution—ROMAN NUMERAL SIGNS

SPRINGFIELD POP.: 3,609

TROY 420 MILES

ADVERTISE HERE! SEEN BY 2,350 PEOPLE PER DAY

KOOL KONES: OVER 1,500 SOLD

BIGGER BETTER BURGER EXIT 253

MILE MARKER 6

45 MPH

INTERSTATE 38

NE 114 ST.

HIGHWAY 571 CLOSED DETOUR 87 STREET TO 66 AVENUE

Solution—HOW SHOULD I MEASURE?

Distance to school	mile
Distance across your desk	inch or foot
Length of your arm	inch
Length of a sidewalk	foot or yard
Amount of milk in a glass	cup
Amount of water in a small pool	gallon
Weight of a car	ton
Weight of a toy car	ounce
Area of your classroom	square foot
Area of a large piece of land	acre

Solution—GOING UP, GOING DOWN

teaspoon, tablespoon, cup, pint, quart, gallon
millimeter, centimeter, decimeter, meter, kilometer
million, billion, trillion, quadrillion, quintillion
day, week, fortnight, month, year, decade, century, millennium

Solution—MEASURE THIS

score	20	years
hand	4 in.	horse's height
gross	12 dozen	pencils
pinch	just a bit	salt
knot	1 nautical mile per hour	ocean liner speed
ream	500 pieces	paper
baker's dozen	13	doughnuts

Solution—WHAT WILL COME NEXT?

11, 17, 23, 29, 35, <u>41</u>, <u>47</u>, <u>53</u>, <u>59</u>	+6
104, 101, 98, 95, 92, <u>89</u>, <u>86</u>, <u>83</u>, <u>80</u>	-3
10, 12, 17, 19, 24, <u>26</u>, <u>31</u>, <u>33</u>, <u>38</u>	+2, +5
3, 9, 12, 36, 39, <u>117</u>, <u>120</u>, <u>360</u>, <u>363</u>	x3, +3
22, 44, 30, 60, 46, <u>92</u>, <u>78</u>, <u>156</u>, <u>142</u>	x2, -14
48, 16, 21, 7, 12, <u>4</u>, <u>9</u>, <u>3</u>, <u>8</u>	÷3, +5

Solution—EXPANDED NUMBERS

$$52,683 = 50,000 + 2,000 + 600 + 80 + 3$$
$$68,144 = 60,000 + 8,000 + 100 + 40 + 4$$
$$226,792 = 200,000 + 20,000 + 6,000 + 700 + 90 + 2$$
$$497,808 = 400,000 + 90,000 + 7,000 + 800 + 0 + 8$$
$$1,939,215 = 1,000,000 + 900,000 + 30,000 + 9,000 + 200 + 10 + 5$$

Message:
THE ZERO IS A PLACE HOLDER.

Solution—HURRY UP!

7:58
3:40
7:18
10:15
11:53
6:00 p.m.

Solution—TIC-TAC-TOE

$\frac{10}{2}$	$\frac{12}{2}$	$\frac{16}{4}$
$\frac{9}{3}$	**6**	$\frac{10}{3}$
$\frac{4}{2}$	$\frac{18}{3}$	$\frac{15}{5}$

3	$\frac{18}{9}$	$\frac{9}{3}$
$\frac{21}{3}$	$\frac{8}{4}$	$\frac{10}{4}$
$\frac{20}{5}$	$\frac{16}{4}$	$\frac{12}{3}$

$\frac{18}{4}$	$\frac{24}{12}$	$\frac{7}{2}$
$\frac{9}{2}$	$\frac{9}{8}$	$\frac{16}{4}$
$4\frac{1}{2}$	$\frac{8}{6}$	$\frac{24}{6}$

$\frac{30}{9}$	$\frac{8}{3}$	$\frac{45}{15}$
$\frac{18}{6}$	$\frac{10}{3}$	$\frac{27}{9}$
$\frac{30}{10}$	$\frac{36}{18}$	$3\frac{1}{3}$

$\frac{11}{4}$	$\frac{22}{8}$	$2\frac{3}{4}$
$\frac{12}{8}$	$\frac{34}{16}$	$\frac{6}{4}$
$\frac{9}{4}$	$\frac{36}{24}$	$\frac{24}{12}$

Solution—A WEB OF NUMBERS

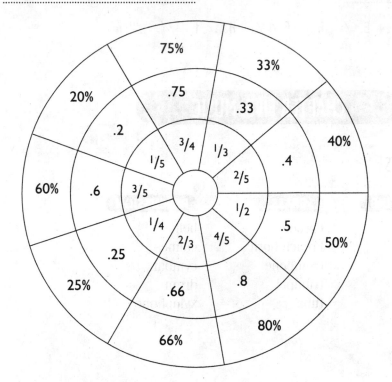

Solution—TRAVELING TIME

The distance from our house to Aunt Jean's house	62.7 mi.
The distance from the Farmer's Market to the park entrance	39.2 mi.
The distance from Aunt Jean's house to town and then to the Farmer's Market	42.4 mi.
The distance from our house to the airport	85.5 mi.

Solution—A TASTY TREAT

Double the recipe:
4 cups flour
$1/2$ cup sugar
2 tablespoons baking powder
1 teaspoon salt
2 eggs
2 cups milk
$1/2$ cup oil
2 cups blueberries

Divide the recipe in half:
1 cup flour
$1/8$ cup sugar
$1/2$ tablespoon baking powder
$1/4$ teaspoon salt
$1/2$ egg (1 egg white)
$1/2$ cup milk
$1/8$ cup oil
$1/2$ cup blueberries

Make 18 muffins:
3 cups flour
$3/8$ cup sugar
$1 1/2$ tablespoons baking powder
3/4 teaspoon salt
$1 1/2$ egg (1 egg plus one egg white)
$1 1/2$ cups milk
$3/8$ cup oil
$1 1/2$ cups blueberries

Solution—Three KINDS OF NUMBERS

A. $^2/_3$ B. $5^1/_4$ C. 2 D. $2^1/_2$ E. $^6/_7$ F. 5 G. $4^2/_3$ H. 4 I. $1^1/_9$ J. $^9/_{10}$

CHAPTER FIVE: MUSIC

Solution—MUSICAL FAMILIES

STRINGS	WOODWIND	BRASS	PERCUSSION
bass	bassoon	cornet	bells
cello	clarinet	French horn	chimes
harp	flute	trombone	cymbal
viola	oboe	trumpet	drum
violin	piccolo	tuba	xylophone

Solution—A MUSICAL WORD

Fits in a lock	KEY
Do this to a car engine	TUNE
A red vegetable	BEET (BEAT)
Peace	HARMONY
You speak with this	VOICE
Drama on a stage	PLAY
You turn this up or down on the TV	VOLUME
A girl's name	MELODY or CAROL
Black	PITCH

Solution—WHAT'S THAT SYMBOL?

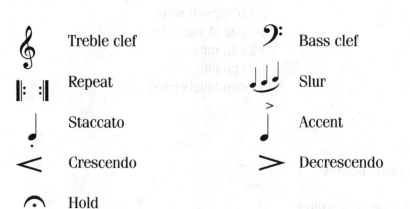

Treble clef · Bass clef

Repeat · Slur

Staccato · Accent

Crescendo · Decrescendo

Hold

Solution—MUSICAL LADDERS

VOICES

soprano
alto
tenor
baritone

GROUPS

solo
duet
trio
quartet

TEMPO

presto
allegro
moderato
andante
largo

Solution—FAMOUS COMPOSERS

MESSAGE:
MOZART, A CHILD PRODIGY, WAS COMPOSING MUSIC AT AGE FOUR.

Solution—PATRIOTIC SONGS

Yankee Doodle	1755	Richard Shuckburg	New England
The Star-Spangled Banner	1814	Francis Scott Key	Baltimore, Maryland
America	1831	Samuel Francis Smith	Andover, Massachusetts
America the Beautiful	1893	Kathryn Lee Bates	Pikes Peak, Colorado
This Land Is Your Land	1940	Woody Guthrie	between Los Angeles and New York

Solution—A COLORFUL PUZZLE

Black	ebony	pitch	raven
Brown	brunette	tan	beige
Purple	lavender	violet	plum
Blue	indigo	aquamarine	navy
Green	emerald	olive	jade
Yellow	maize	lemon	canary
Orange	tangerine	pumpkin	copper
Red	crimson	ruby	scarlet
Pink	salmon	coral	carnation
White	oyster	ivory	alabaster

Solution—WHAT CAN AN ARTIST USE?

1. crayon
2. pen
3. paint
4. chalk
5. oil paint
6. tempera
7. pastel
8. pencil
9. watercolor
10. poster paint
11. wax
12. charcoal

Solution—20th CENTURY ARTISTS

1. Henry Moore
2. Alexander Calder
3. Edward Steichen
4. Dorothea Lange
5. Norman Rockwell
6. Georgia O'Keeffe
7. Pablo Picasso
8. Jackson Pollock
9. Andrew Wyeth
10. Roy Lichtenstein

Solution—RENAISSANCE PAINTERS

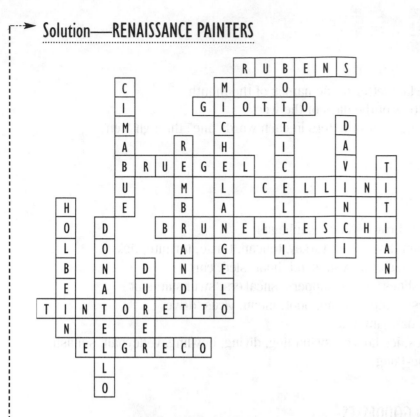

CHAPTER SEVEN: THINKING SKILLS/PROBLEM SOLVING

Solution—WHAT ELSE CAN I BE?

POSSIBLE CAREERS:

HISTORY—teacher, writer, museum curator, archaeologist, researcher; work at a living history museum, historical society, historical museum

GEOGRAPHY—cartographer, surveyor, teacher, researcher; work in a city planning department, government, travel industry

CIVICS—attorney, politician, teacher; work in government, especially State Department or Congress

READING—editor, writer, researcher, librarian, storyteller, translator; work in publishing

WRITING—writer, reporter, editor, screenwriter, advertising copywriter; work in public relations

SPEECH—TV/radio announcer, attorney, speech therapist, translator, sign language interpreter; work in communications

MATH—teacher, engineer, accountant, office manager, chief financial officer, city manager, bank teller, statistician, scientist, computer systems analyst; work in data processing, insurance, marketing, investments

SCIENCE—engineer, doctor, dentist, veterinarian, pharmacist, researcher, chemist, physicist, astronomer, forester, meteorologist, medical technologist, oceanographer, teacher

ART—artist, museum curator, architect, fashion designer, photographer, art supply store owner, interior designer, woodworker, teacher, gallery owner

MUSIC—musician, teacher, dancer, choreographer, music store owner, music therapist, director, instrument maker, songwriter; work in the recording industry, radio, orchestra

Solution—FINISH IT

y, y, h, l, y, e, y, t, r, r, r, r—the last letter of the names of the months
S, M, T, W, T, F, S—the first letters of the days of the week
3, 3, 5, 4, 4, 3, 5, 5, 4, 3—the number of letters in each word "one" through "ten"

Solution—THINK FAST

SOME POSSIBILITIES:
Body parts—eye, ear, elbow, eyebrow, eyelid, esophagus
Animals—tiger, toad, Tasmanian devil, tapir, turkey, toucan, turtle, termite, tick
Getting around—cab, taxi, bus, legs, car, van, semi, boat, sled, cart
Clothing—shorts, shirt, skirt, shoes, socks, slippers, sneakers, swimsuit, suit
Computer terms—mouse, crash, chip, backup, boot, menu, virus, drive
Foods—egg, oil, nut, fig, yam, oat, jam, tea
Sports—basketball, gymnastics, ice hockey, swimming, diving, bowling, volleyball, squash, weight lifting, racquetball, Ping-Pong

Solution—GREEK AND ROMAN GODDESSES

Solution—GREEK AND ROMAN GODS

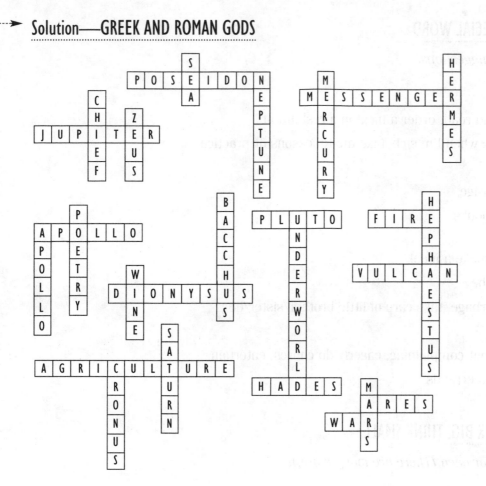

Solution— WHO WORKS WHERE?

Paige — bookstore
Carol — music store
Starr — planetarium
Bill — credit card company
Rose — flower shop
Colt — ranch
Amber — natural history museum
Will — law office

Solution—AN INTERESTING PLACE

1. birds
2. dogs
3. poultry
4. solar system model
5. fish
6. cooks, food
7. horses
8. dress-up, masks
9. plants
10. art, historical objects

Solution—A SPECIAL WORD

Here are some suggestions:

Make dinner

Open a book and read, order a meal in a restaurant

Take care of me when I'm sick, take me to lessons or practice

Hug, heal

Educate, encourage

Return library books

Mop the floor, make a meal

Offer to help, obey

Take out the garbage, take care of little brother/sister/dog

Hug, help

Eat meals without complaining, eagerly do chores, entertain

Rake leaves, run errands

Solution—THINK BIG, THINK SMALL

One possibility for each (There are many more.):

	NARROWER	**BROADER**
airplanes	747	transportation
beans	green beans	food
bird	blue jay	animals
house	cabin	buildings
cake	angel food	desserts
shirt	T-shirt	clothes
coin	dime	money
swimming	side stroke	sports
rain	drizzle	weather
light bulb	fluorescent	illumination

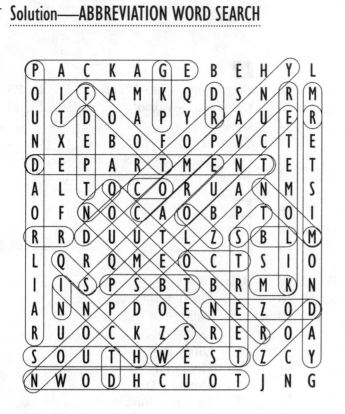

Subject Index

Skills Index